KIM JONG IL

ON THE ART OF OPERA

Talk to Creative Workers in the
Field of Art and Literature
September 4-6, 1974

University Press of the Pacific
Honolulu, Hawaii

Kim Jong Il   On the Art of Opera

by
Kim Jong Il

ISBN 0-89875-203-5

Reprinted from the 1990 edition

University Press of the Pacific
Honolulu, Hawaii
http://www.UniversityPressofthePacific.com

CONTENTS

Three years have passed since the creation and first performance of the revolutionary opera *The Sea of Blood*.

I am delighted to be meeting again you, the creative workers in the field of art and literature, who have, by taking an active part in the opera revolution over recent years, made a significant contribution to the development of opera art, and to be talking to you, recollecting the creative work done in those years.

It was in July 1971 that we adapted the classic drama *The Sea of Blood*, which was created in the flames of the anti-Japanese revolutionary struggle, into a revolutionary opera of our own style, and gave the premiere of it in the presence of the great leader. This was an event of great significance in the development of art and literature in our country.

The creation and public performance of the revolutionary opera *The Sea of Blood* proclaimed to the world the birth of a new style of opera, the *Sea of Blood*-style opera, which is fundamentally different from conventional operas. Since then steady progress has been made in the opera revolution in our country. The creation of the revolutionary opera *The Sea of Blood* was a historic turning point, the breaking of the old pattern that had remained in the field of opera for many years and the ushering in of a new era of revolutionary opera.

In the course of creating the revolutionary opera *The Sea of Blood* we gained valuable experiences and, on the basis of this, staged the revolutionary opera *The Flower Girl* which, in a little over a year, was adapted from the classic drama of the same name; then we created, in succession, the revolutionary operas, *Tell O Forest, A True Daughter of the Party* and *Song*

1

of Mt. Kumgang. For their high ideological and noble artistic qualities, the revolutionary operas created in the course of our opera revolution have aroused the great admiration not only of our people but also of the peoples of many other countries across the world. This is a rich fruit of our Party's policy on the opera revolution. The golden age of opera in our country began in the first half of the 1970s.

Having reviewed the successes and experiences gained in the opera revolution, I will speak about some problems arising in further developing opera art.

I. THE TIMES AND OPERA

1) THE OPERA REVOLUTION IS A REQUIREMENT OF THE TIMES

Opera art reflects the times, and its change and development are governed by the era. The operas of the feudal and capitalist days represented and served those periods.

Ours is a new historical era when the popular masses have emerged as the masters of their destiny and of the world and are making history and shaping their own destiny. This period requires a new type of opera to serve the popular masses.

The operas which were created in the exploitative society contain the socio-historical and ideological and artistic limitations of that age, so they do not accord with the thoughts and feelings of our contemporaries who are building socialism and communism, nor do they cater to their cultural needs. Although a number of changes have been evident in operas in the past, they were essentially mere reforms within the bounds of bourgeois opera. The newly-emergent bourgeoisie was opposed to the operas that had been serving feudal lords, so they advocated "human rights" and "liberty". However, when they themselves became the ruling class, they made opera serve those who were rich. By preaching a longing for the good old days and class cooperation by means of opera, the successive ruling classes used it as a means of pacifying the discontent of the people with the exploitative system. Therefore, opera remained for a long time as a form of entertainment and a means of money-making, and a tool for spreading illusions about emperors, God, power and gold.

From the artistic point of view, the operas of bygone days do not accord with the requirements of the masses of our times. The forms and methods of portrayal of conventional operas, which were made to cater to the tastes of the exploiting classes, contain many aspects that do not appeal to the tastes and feelings of the people of our times. Our people today do not like amorphous lyrics, complicated rhythms, recitatives that are neither songs nor speeches, outmoded stage-settings and other stereotyped methods of portrayal. Without eliminating such outmoded patterns we cannot produce a true opera that reflects the aspirations and needs of the masses. In order to overcome the socio-historical, ideological and artistic limitations of opera art and create an opera of a new style that reflects the aspirations and desires of the people of the Juche age, we must conduct a revolution in all domains of opera—the content and form, the system and method of creation.

Conducting a revolution in opera is also a pressing need for the development of art and literature in our country. Opera is a mixed art that integrates poems, music, dance and fine arts. On the basis of music it presents to the people a beautiful and noble life and teaches them a lot about their life and struggle. That is why everyone likes opera. As a mixed art that incorporates all the forms of theatrical art it constitutes a criterion for evaluating the level of a country's art and has a major effect on developing theatrical art in general.

In accordance with the line of building Juche national culture, strenuous efforts were made in our country after liberation to create a new style of national opera which is national in form and democratic in content and, in the course of this, operas of various forms were created. These operas, being products of their own efforts and talents, were a source of pride for our artists who had not created even one opera worth mentioning before liberation due to the colonial policy of obliterating our national culture pursued by the Japanese imperialists. However, the operas produced during the periods of peaceful, democratic development, the Fatherland Liberation War and postwar reconstruction were based mainly on legends or historical tales, and their forms failed to cater to the tastes and sentiments of our people in many respects.

The reason for the defects revealed in the creation of national operas in the past was that some artists and writers were steeped in outdated ideas. Those who retained the tendency to return to the past, claiming that the national opera should, as a matter of course, be *Changkuk* (a classical Korean opera—Tr.) consisting of *pansori*[1], were opposed to modernizing *Changkuk* as required by the period; those who were infected with flunkeyism and dogmatism, claiming that operas should naturally be of a Western style, tried to copy the pattern of Western operas. They did not perceive the magnificent reality of the Chollima age[2] vibrant with miraculous events and innovations, but tried to produce operas which dealt only with the lives of emperors and princesses of the past or love affairs.

In postwar years when flunkeyism, dogmatism and the tendency to return to the past were rife, our Party launched a powerful struggle to establish Juche in all fields of art and literature, including opera. In the course of this struggle the tendency to deal exclusively with mythical, legendary and historical themes was overcome and operas began to depict the lives of our people who were working for the revolution and socialist construction. The replacement of the anachronistically obsolete themes, that had suited the period when people wore horsehair hats and rode donkeys, with socialist events in operas marked a milestone in the development of art and literature in our country.

However, no such change as took place in the content of opera was evident in its form. Because still then the creative workers considered it impossible to produce operas without arias or recitatives, nobody thought of effecting a radical change in the form of opera. In consequence, although an innovation had been made in the content of opera, its form still remained within the framework of the old pattern. This resulted in a discrepancy between the content and the form. *Under the Sunshine,* produced by the then State Opera Troupe, for instance, was outmoded in its form in spite of its revolutionary content.

In art the form must undergo continuous change to suit its new content. As the form expresses the content and is determined by it, it should, if it does not agree with the new content, be changed accordingly. Only through the unity of content and form in art can the ideological and artistic qualities be integrated properly. That is why a revolution had to be effected in the form of opera.

An opera revolution to break the old pattern of conventional opera and create a new style of opera was a pressing demand that brooked no further delay. The opera of a new style could only be completed when the old pattern, which had been polished and hardened in a way best suited to the tastes and feelings of the exploiting classes over a long period, was discarded and a new form was created to suit the socialist content.

Our Party put forward the policy of doing away with everything obsolete that suited the interests and tastes of the exploiting classes in all fields of art and literature and of building Juche art and literature which agreed with the requirements of our age and with the nature of the working class, and conducted a revolution firstly in the sphere of the cinema, one of the powerful means of educating the masses, and then in the sphere of the opera.

2) PRINCIPLES MUST BE OBSERVED IN THE OPERA REVOLUTION

Sound principles are necessary in the opera revolution. Although it is a pressing need of the age, the opera revolution cannot be carried out successfully unless it is guided by sound principles. In order to effect a revolution in opera and create operas which really meet the aspirations and needs of the people and age, the undertaking must be guided strictly by revolutionary principles.

Establishing Juche in opera art is a fundamental principle that must always be adhered to in the opera revolution.

Establishing Juche in opera art means solving all the problems relating to the creation of operas to meet the interests of the revolution in one's own country and of one's own people and to suit the specific situation in one's own country and the sentiments of one's nation.

Our opera art must be subordinated to the interests of the Korean revolution and contribute to it. Only opera art which resolutely champions the interests of the revolution and implements Party lines can be loved by the people and become a powerful weapon for encouraging them in the revolution and construction.

Operas must be created to suit the specific situation in one's country and to accord with the feelings of one's people.

Socio-historical conditions vary from country to country and so do the people's feelings and tastes. Those who create operas must have a good knowledge of the specific situation in their country and the sentiments of their nation and depict them accurately. In this way they will truthfully describe the lives of people who are shaping their destiny independently and creatively, in an artistic form that people like and enjoy.

In order to establish Juche in opera, all the problems involved in the creation of opera must be solved creatively on an independent basis.

Art and literature are a creative undertaking to portray independent and creative people and their lives. All problems in the creation of art and literature must be solved independently and creatively to conform with the tastes and feelings of one's people and to serve the interests of the revolution in one's own country and of one's own people. The opera revolution is something no one has ever undertaken before. There was no ready-made theory aspects of which we could adopt for our opera revolution. We had to solve all the problems that arose in the opera revolution in our own way according to our own beliefs and judgement and on an independent and creative basis.

In order to establish Juche in opera art, we must express socialist content in national form. This means changing the content and form of opera as required by the Juche idea. In other words, we must do away with the outmoded, reactionary content and form of the past which catered to the tastes of the exploiting classes and replace them with content which is revolutionary and socialist and deals with the people's struggle to realize their independence. We must also create popular and national forms suited to the tastes and feelings of the people of our age.

The main aspect of the innovation of the content and form

of opera is the innovation of the content. The value of an opera is determined by its content. No matter how gorgeous the stage is and no matter how well the singers sing, an opera with poor content cannot win the acclamation of the audience. An opera with sound and noble content alone is entitled to be one for the people and can inspire them to the creation of a new life.

Our opera art has a noble mission to assist in the modelling of the whole society on the Juche idea. In order to perform the noble mission it has assumed before the times and the revolution, above all its content must be revolutionary and popular.

Our people's life and struggle are full of events that should be dealt with by operas. Important problems in our people's struggle for national liberation, class emancipation, man's emancipation and other endeavours to realize independence must be raised and solved in the people's interests. Only then can our operas, as Juche humanics contributing to the accomplishment of the cause of independence for the popular masses, fulfil its duty to the times.

If an opera is to be revolutionary and popular it must meet the requirements of the present era and accord with the thoughts and feelings of the people.

To this end, it must represent the people's lives and struggle properly as an art which is struggling together with the people and advancing with the times.

An opera can deal with a legend or an historical event. Regardless of the life and the period it is based upon, it must contribute to teaching our contemporaries how to live, work and fight.

We must ensure that the content of opera is completely free from outmoded elements which are feudalistic and capitalistic and that it is revolutionary and popular in all aspects so that it contributes to the struggle to realize independence for the popular masses.

The form of opera must also be transformed to suit the aesthetic tastes of the people. A work of progressive and revolutionary art and literature is characterized by perfect unity between a sound content and a refined form that accord with the requirements of the period and the people's aspirations. However excellent its content is, art whose form does not agree with the people's aspirations and desires has no value whatsoever. Only opera in which revolutionary and socialist content is in harmony with elegant, beautiful national form can be opera truly for the people.

Our opera is for the Party, for the working class, and for the people, and serves them. Loyalty to the Party, to the working class and to the people is the lifeblood of our opera. If opera is devoid of this loyalty, it has no lifeblood. In the creation of operas we must steadfastly adhere to the principle of loyalty to the Party, to the working class and to the people.

In order to observe this principle in the creation of operas, we must embody in operas the Party's lines and policies correctly and portray our reality, in which the Party's policies are embodied, truthfully. In addition, we must establish the line of the working class correctly in the creation of operas. If not, it would be impossible to produce works that represent the interests and aspirations of the working class. Whatever themes we may deal with in the operas we produce, we must hold fast to the principle of loyalty to the Party and to the working class.

Adhering to the principle of loyalty to the people is an important guarantee for ensuring that an opera truly serves the people. In order to hold fast to this principle in the creation of operas, the lives of people who aspire to independence should be portrayed realistically and profoundly in a form they can understand easily and accept willingly. However excellent its content is, an opera the form of which is outdated, complicated and incomprehensible to the people cannot be loved by them. The operas of the past were not loved by the people both because their content was anti-popular and particularly because they took the form of arias or recitatives which were unattractive and incomprehensible to our people.

For an opera to be popular, arias and recitatives must be replaced by popular songs and orchestral music which are comprehensible to everyone and capable of being sung by everyone.

Some people say that popular songs and orchestral music reduce the artistic quality of operas. Such people are opposed to art for the people. Being opposed to popular songs allegedly for the sake of artistic quality is an expression of the tendency towards art for art's sake. Genuine art is popular art. Only an opera that has noble content harmonized with a popular form of music, such as stanzaic songs, can be understood easily and loved by the people.

If an opera is to accord with the emotions and aesthetic tastes of the popular masses, it must accurately reflect national characteristics. The characteristics of different nations are based on their differences in thoughts and feelings, way of life, culture and customs. For that reason, for art and literature to portray life realistically they must reflect national characteristics, and these find peculiar expression in the life of the people of that country.

Depicting our people's life and the national feelings truthfully is a basic method of reflecting our national characteristics. In order to give proper operatic expression to our national characteristics, we must sustain our people's national life and feelings evolved over a long historical course and realistically describe our people's beautiful and noble mental and moral traits and worthwhile life that are being formed in the course of conducting the revolution and construction. Along with this, we must discover and make the best use of the melodies of folk songs and the movement patterns of folk dance created and refined by our people over the ages, develop our national musical instruments and further perfect singing and the playing of instruments in our own style. In the field of stage art, too, we must introduce the latest achievements of modern science and technology while preserving our national stage art, and thus present a fresh operatic stage.

Combining ideological quality and artistic quality is an important principle in the creation of operas. Opera art, whose mission is to educate people in a revolutionary way, should be not only high in ideological quality but also high in artistic quality. An opera with high ideological quality but low artistic quality or vice versa cannot fulfil its function of cognition and education. While conducting the opera revolution, we boldly smashed the outdated pattern of conventional operas and created operas of a new type, *Sea of Blood*-style operas in which the ideological and artistic qualities are in perfect harmony.

In the creation of operas the principles of the speed campaign[3] and collectivism must be rigidly maintained.

It is only when creative workers and artists, in support of the policy of the speed campaign set by the Party, give priority to political work at each stage of their creative work and launch a lightning operation[4] and employ finish-one-by-one tactics, that they can produce perfect operas in a short time. Our practical experience in the opera revolution tells us clearly that conducting the speed campaign is a revolutionary principle of doing creative work which ensures the highest level of ideological and artistic qualities of works of art and literature and an extremely rapid development of art and literature, as the situation demands.

The principle of collectivism ensures that the collective carries out all tasks, however difficult, by its own efforts, helping and leading one another forward under the communist slogan of "One for all and all for one!" and that the people undergo steady, revolutionary training in the course of this. By applying the principle of collectivism in the creation of operas, creative workers and artists must strengthen the ideological unity and cohesion of the collective, transform themselves into revolutionaries and assimilate themselves to the working class.

3) THE *SEA OF BLOOD*-STYLE OPERA IS AN OPERA OF A NEW STYLE

There is a variety of operatic styles. Operatic style is the manner and form in which songs and orchestra and various other means of portrayal are employed in creating an opera. Different operatic styles are determined according to which means of portrayal is employed and how it is used.

Operatic styles have changed according to the times and nation. Within the limitations of ideology and the standard of music and art of the period, they have been influenced by the cultural traditions, sentiments and aesthetic tastes of nations. *Changkuk* that was produced in our country in the past was different from the Beijing opera and Western opera. The style of creation of art and literature and national characteristics are different matters, but they are closely related. Even the same style of art is adopted and employed in different ways by different nations.

Different social classes also have different effects on the characteristics of the style of opera. Just as different classes have different attitudes towards life and different views on it, so their manners and forms of representing life by means of art are different.

Since the operatic style is governed by the period, assumes national characteristics and follows the requirements of classes, we should naturally create a new style of opera which conforms with the requirements of our times, our people's aspirations and the intrinsic nature of the working class. The operatic style of feudalism or capitalism cannot serve the creation of operas for the working class who are now building socialism and communism, nor can the imitation of foreign things help in producing operas that cater to the aesthetic tastes and feelings of our people.

We must transform and develop opera art in our own way as we do when solving the problems that arise in the other fields of the revolution and construction.

In order to develop opera in our own fashion, we must free ourselves from the Western style of opera and create a new style which accords with the characteristics of our nation and suits the aesthetic tastes of our people today.

By setting the policy of conducting the opera revolution and working hard to create operas of our own style, we have produced a perfect revolutionary opera, *The Sea of Blood,* an adaptation of the classic, dramatic masterpiece of the same name. This new revolutionary opera, which has been produced in our own fashion and form, is evoking a positive response from our people and the peoples of many other countries.

All the songs in *Sea of Blood*-style operas are composed in stanzas. The sweeping introduction of the stanzaic form was the turning point in eliminating the outmoded, anti-popular

14

elements of the operas of the past and creating original operas in our own way. The stanzaic composition of all opera songs provides the possibility of portraying the ideological content in great depth and breadth through a succinct structure and making the songs beautiful and easy to sing. In conventional operas arias and recitatives were regarded as a basic means of portrayal, and it was considered impossible, without arias and recitatives, to link the music and the drama and create beautiful and refined operas.

Although opera is an art which combines music and drama, songs play a fundamental role in making opera art a beautiful and noble art. However, establishing the relations between characters and weaving the drama with recitatives, which are difficult to sing and awkward to listen to, does not conform with our people's tastes and feelings.

Songs must always serve the people, and they should be composed in such a way that anybody can understand and sing them. Art for art's sake is pointless. In order to make opera art a truly popular art, we must discard the recitative and make all operatic songs stanzaic. In *Sea of Blood*-style operas not only the recitatives but also the arias and all other songs have been replaced by stanzaic songs.

Introducing stanzaic songs is important in improving the ideological and artistic qualities of an opera. Opera music is valuable in that it expresses noble content in beautiful melodies and touches the people's heartstrings. Because a stanzaic song integrates poetic words and beautiful melodies, it can express the characters' thoughts and feelings intensively in a simpler structure than an aria or a recitative. A stanzaic song can express the characters' thoughts, feelings and psychological state delicately, ensure the effective depiction of the situation that surrounds them, and provide freedom of interaction between characters. As you can see, stanzaic songs can improve the ideological and artistic qualities of a work by fulfilling functions which were beyond the capability of the vocal music of conventional operas.

The introduction of stanzaic songs into opera music is of great significance in enhancing the popular character of operas, in that these songs are simple and comprehensible to the people. In our new operas, all the songs are composed in stanzas which are beautiful, gentle and overflowing with national sentiments, so everyone enjoys singing these songs.

In *Sea of Blood*-style operas the *pangchang* (off-stage song—Tr.) has been introduced as an important means of operatic portrayal. The introduction of the *pangchang* is another change in the development of operas. The *pangchang* plays an important role in depicting the events taking place on the stage and the characters' thoughts and feelings. It was a rule in conventional operas to organize and develop the drama only through songs sung by the characters and orchestral music. The newly-created *pangchang* describes the times, situation and the inmost world and actions of the characters in an objective way, conveys the inmost thoughts and feelings of the characters, provides links between the stage and the audience, and helps the characters to perform well. In addition it forms a grand chorus with the song of the character on the stage, and in some cases the members of the *pangchang* group appear on the stage and take an active part in the drama. The introduction of the *pangchang* has provided our operas with a powerful means of portrayal not present in the operas of the past and has broadened the scope of operatic portrayal beyond measure.

Dance is an indispensable means of portrayal in *Sea of Blood*-style operas. Although there were dances in the operas of the past, they were not interwoven closely with the storyline but appeared on the stage, as incidental to a scene. So they were not used as an indispensable means of portrayal. In our new operas, however, dance, as an essential element of portrayal which is interwoven closely with the storyline, has become a powerful means of portrayal that describes the background of the times, the thoughts and feelings of the principal character and all the characters' aspirations and desires.

In *Sea of Blood*-style operas, the role of stage art has also changed. Our new stage art combining sides, lighting and setting has broken the old pattern of stage setting that had been hardened over a long period of time. In the past it was considered possible to produce operas only with stage settings which described life through a few stereotyped acts and scenes. That was why, although they admitted the need for realistic settings portraying the environment of the characters, creative workers portrayed the surroundings in static state only through the back part of the stage and the background and made it a rule that breaks must occur between acts, thus interrupting the drama. *Sea of Blood*-style operas have smashed the previous idea of fixed stage settings and depict the environment realistically in three dimensions, unfolding the flow of the change of environment without interruption and organizing the drama in such a way as to give the audience the impression of real life.

Sea of Blood-style operas have also opened up a new phase in dramaturgy. The new operas employ stanzaic songs, capable of admirably expressing the characters' thoughts and feelings in a complete musical image, as the main means of musical dramaturgy, and these not only help to describe characters but also make it easy for the audience to understand the story, the relations between the characters and the flow of the drama. Moreover the music, acting, dance, stage art and all the other means of portrayal are subordinated to

17

describing the characters in conformity with the logic of life, and their functions and roles are enhanced considerably, so that the level of artistic quality of operas can be raised still higher. This shows that *Sea of Blood*-style operas are totally different from the operas of the past which, regarding the recitative as a means of musical dramaturgy, gave prominence to the dramatic development of the music, which depended on leitmotiv.

In our new operas all the means of portrayal are combined and harmonized on the basis of stanzaic songs. Because the lyrics in the librettos of the new style of operas are all composed in a fixed form of verse, all the music is stanzaic. Consequently, the acting of the characters as well as the dance is tuned to the music, and the stage settings and the backgrounds change with the flow of the songs. The unity of orchestra, dance and stage settings on the basis of stanzaic songs, and the development of the drama accompanied by dancing and the change of the scenes on the basis of stanzaic songs, represent precisely the *Sea of Blood*-style of opera. The *Sea of Blood*-style of opera consisting of stanzaic songs and the *pangchang* of our own fashion, and dancing and stage art of our own style constitutes a completely new style of opera never seen before in the history of opera.

We must consolidate the successes achieved in the creation of new operas, *Sea of Blood*-style operas, and continue to develop them.

2. THE LIBRETTO

1) THE LIBRETTO IS THE IDEOLOGICAL AND ARTISTIC BASIS OF AN OPERA

An excellent libretto is essential for the creation of an opera which touches the people's heartstrings.

The seed and theme of an opera, and its characters and storyline, are all indicated in the libretto; the music, dance and stage art, too, are determined by the libretto. Only when a valuable subject is dealt with in a libretto and portrayed skilfully in a way best suited to the characteristics of opera can, on this basis, an opera of high ideological and artistic qualities be created. You must not rely solely on the music and neglect the libretto simply because opera is an art based on music. It was a wrong tendency of the era when opera was regarded as a means of pleasure to give prominence to a few pieces of music while neglecting the libretto.

Writers must have a correct understanding of the importance of the libretto in the creation of opera and concentrate their efforts on writing good librettos.

Operas make an active contribution to the ideological and aesthetic education of people. Therefore, librettos must be deep and rich in their content. Only such librettos can provide the soil for creative thinking and imagination as well as the basis of wonderful songs, orchestral music, dances and stage art.

In order to create a libretto with deep and rich ideological content, the seed of the work must be well selected.

As the nucleus of a work, the seed guarantees its ideological and artistic value. The depth of the ideological content and the educational value of a libretto depend on the seed. In creative work, therefore, the main attention must always be paid to the selection of the right seed. If a librettist starts to write without selecting a proper seed, mixing up the seed and the theme, he cannot produce a good libretto.

The seed of a work in itself is not a theme or a thought but the ideological kernel which underlies and determines them. Only through his study and analysis of life from his class position and his aesthetic point of view can a writer grasp an ideological kernel of life which inspires him to creation: that is the seed. If the writer, failing to grasp the ideological kernel of life, regards a sphere of life or some event in life as his theme and starts writing on the basis of that, he cannot produce a work with a proper seed.

Writers must eliminate the practice of identifying the seed with the theme or of writing after selecting an unworthy seed. They must develop their creative work in depth only when they have chosen a meaningful seed and fully grasped its meaning.

The struggle and life of our people, who are working for the revolution and construction, contain a lot of meaningful seeds that deserve operatic depiction. Many seeds for the creation of operas of high ideological and artistic qualities can be found in the heroic struggle of the anti-Japanese revolutionary fighters, who waged an arduous struggle for many years for the liberation of the fatherland, the heroic struggle of the valiant soldiers of our People's Army and our people who, having inherited the brilliant revolutionary traditions of the anti-Japanese struggle, fought bravely during the Fatherland Liberation War, and in today's magnificent reality of advancing in the spirit of Chollima spurred on by the speed campaign and in our people's worthwhile life. Writers must penetrate the reality and select seeds for operas that can provide the people with revolutionary education.

In selecting seeds it is important on which stand and with what attitude a writer views life and how he studies it. He must not neglect the life of an ordinary man or a small event in selecting a meaningful seed, while paying attention only to the life of a famous man or a major event. Valuable seeds can be found not only in the life of a famous man or a major event but also in the life of an ordinary man or in a small event. If the life of an ordinary man reflects the needs of the period and the people's aspirations, it is sure to contain the meaningful ideological kernel of life.

The revolutionary opera *The Flower Girl* exposes the contradictions of the exploitative society through the life of Ggot Bun and her family, who are forced to live the life of servants for generations on account of two *mal* of foxtail millet which they owe to a landlord. The opera is implanted with a profound seed that her flower basket of sorrow and filial duty becomes the flower basket of struggle and revolution. Precisely from this seed is derived the theme of the destiny of a nation that has lost its sovereignty and is living in misery. The development of this theme clarifies the idea that revolution is the only way to liberate one's nation and oneself. As you see, the seed of the revolutionary opera *The Flower Girl* is meaningful and profound, but the life which elucidates the seed is commonplace. It could be found everywhere in our country's rural areas before liberation.

Experience tells us that you must not try to find seeds only in important lives or major events simply because the seeds of works should be of great social significance.

Works of art and literature can and must portray gigantic historical events and the lives of well-known men. Even in that case, a philosophical seed must be selected from concrete and realistic events and described in depth from various angles. Only then is it possible to reach a momentous conclusion and clarify a profound thought.

Whether the event depicted in an opera is big or small and whether the event is contemporary or historical, the seed must always contain worthy human problems raised in life as well as the aspirations and desires of the people. In other words, the seed of an opera must be capable of providing a solution to the problem of the destiny of the popular masses who are struggling for an independent and creative life and to the problems of national liberation, class emancipation and man's freedom. In all cases only a seed which can give a profound answer to the question of the destiny of an independent man and his political integrity can provide a definite guarantee for the creation of an opera of high ideological quality and noble artistic value.

In order to write a libretto with profound and rich ideological content, it is essential to depict the personalities of the principal and other characters skilfully.

The personality of a character is fundamental to the development of the seed. All the means of portrayal, such as the event, conflict, storyline and composition, play an important role in the development of the seed but, of all these, the depiction of their personalities, especially the characterization of the hero, is decisive. The principal character is essential for the development of the seed. For that reason, characterization must naturally be focussed on the hero. The seed can come into full bloom only when the relations between the characters are properly established around the hero, when the line of action of all the characters is linked closely with that of the hero, and when their personalities are depicted well in accordance with the logic of life.

A contemporary hero who appears in a work of art or literature must be a typical, independent and creative man who lives and works with an attitude befitting the master of the revolution and construction. The time is gone when the feudal emperors, aristocrats and millionaires were given prominence in operas.

Ours is an era when the popular masses are struggling to defend independence. Operas of our era must raise the question of man's independence and of independent man, and give a full answer to the question of people's political integrity through a typical man who shapes his own destiny independently and creatively.

In order to write a libretto with profound and rich ideological content, you must write it to suit the characteristics of opera.

For this, the storyline must be solid and yet concise.

Each genre of art has its peculiar way of describing life. Like cinema and drama, opera is an art which portrays life dramatically, but the method of weaving the storyline is different.

In an opera it is difficult to establish many storylines and stage a lot of scenes as in a film or in a drama. Certainly, *Sea of Blood*-style operas employ the *pangchang* and a new stage art which make it possible to portray many aspects of life in great breadth. But this does not allow a freedom to describe life without the limitations of time and place as in a film or novel. Since opera is an art which describes life by means of music, the plot must be composed properly and the storyline woven solidly and yet in a concise manner so as to deal with life concisely and intensively.

Weaving a solid and concise storyline means composing the drama in a way that vividly shows the characters' personalities and the process of the development of the relations between them. The storyline is not an array of various aspects of life, nor is it a mere connection of events. It is the process of the inevitable development of the characters' personalities and life. Only when the storyline is solid and concise can the opera express its theme and thought clearly and weave the drama musically. If the storyline lacks solidness and is confused by various aspects of life and events, the drama will be desultory and entangling, and the musical representation will be difficult. Since the clarity of dramatic structure depends on how the storyline is woven, the storyline must be solid and concise, as required by the characteristics of opera.

The storyline must not include every event and episode simply because they are interesting. The plot of an opera must be made up of only such selected events and episodes as essential for elucidating the theme and thought, for describing the characters' personalities and their lives and for describing the relationship between them. This is the way to compose a plot properly.

In order to compose a storyline for an opera, the major event must be selected and combined with other events carefully.

The major event is the basis on which the lines of action of the principal and other characters are linked, the relationship between them established and the conflicts developed. It acts directly on elucidating the theme and thought of a work. Only when the selected events spread from the trunk of the major event like tree branches growing from a single trunk can the storyline be compact. If the plot is a mechanical assembly of different events, then the story is incoherent, and the drama

24

cannot be realistic and dynamic.

In order to weld the major event and other events harmoniously in the storyline, the relations between the characters centring around the major event must be established properly and co-ordinated with the relations between the characters around the other events, and then woven to conform with the logic of life. The storyline unfolds with the establishment and development of the relations between the characters in the course of the occurrence and development of events, so the composition should be done in such a way that the relations between the characters and the process of the development of their personalities make up the full storyline.

Confrontation and struggle between the characters who are in contradiction are the motive force developing the storyline.

A proper establishment of the relations between the positive and negative characters and a skilful arrangement of these relations can portray their conflicts and struggle clearly and propel the storyline dynamically and in a tense atmosphere. The stronger the desire of the positive and negative characters to achieve their ends, the more intense their confrontation and struggle can be, and the greater momentum the storyline can gain. Whether or not the confrontation and conflict are sharp depends on the social relations they represent. The confrontation which represents an antagonistic social relationship should be sharp, but the confrontation which represents the lives of the working people in a socialist society should not be extreme. Under certain circumstances strongly dramatic works can be produced even though they do not contain any direct confrontation or clash between positive and negative characters. It is old-fashioned dramaturgy to require sharp antagonism and conflict without considering specific social relations.

The storyline of an opera must be dramatic, elastic and tense. In other words, the dramatic sequence must not distract the audience from the opera.

To this end, the characters must be closely interrelated and their relations tinged with emotions and variety in the course of the dramatic development, until the climax is reached.

The climax is the moment when a qualitative change takes place in the characters' personalities and in the dramatic development; it is the point where the conflicts culminate in an intensive exposition of the theme and thought of the work. When composing a storyline, the writer must calculate accurately where to place the climax and how to bring the dramatic tension to a head. When the climax coincides with the critical point of the contradiction as an inevitable consequence of the life and events, so far, the storyline will be automatically elastic and tense.

For the storyline to be woven in this way, the emotions must be arranged well.

We cannot think of the organization of the drama apart from the organization of emotions. Particularly in operas events can be shown emotionally only when they develop along the line of the emotions of the characters. No matter how acute the conflicts involved in the events are and how serious the action is, it is difficult to make them impressive unless the characters' emotional experience of the events and the emotions on which the action is based are described delicately. It is only when emotions of various colours that flow out from the experiences of the characters in every scene and at every moment of the development of the drama are represented delicately that the storyline can be elastic and tense and that the organization of the drama can be a delicate organization of emotion.

For the dramatic organization to correspond with the emotional organization, the scenes must be established and developed along the line of the emotions of the characters. Then, the emotions of the songs can be sustained and the emotions of the scenes strengthened. Opera songs can overflow with emotions only when they are based on the accumulation of the characters' emotions; and the scenes can be full of emotions to suit the characteristics of the opera only when they are established and developed along the line of the characters' emotions.

Realistic dramatic composition in line with the developing storyline is an important factor in making dramatic delineation delicate emotional delineation. Dramatism emanates from the acuteness of the conflicts involved in the events and from the depth of the characters' experience of that acuteness. The aim of the realistic composition of drama is always to draw the audience deep into the world of the production so that they can digest the emotional content of the opera still better. However, the tension of the events must not be stepped up artificially, nor the characters' experience emphasized illogically. Artificial tension and seriousness have nothing in common with realistic dramatism. Dramatism must be created in accordance with the logic of life and emotions, and not for its own sake. In order to achieve realistic dramatism, the characters' experience of the events must be depicted in depth.

In an opera the description of life must be delicate and rich, while the storyline should be compact and concise.

The delicate and rich description of life can show the characters' personalities and events in sharp contrast and in a variety of ways so as to strengthen the drama.

Not everything should be depicted in song simply because

27

opera art depicts life musically. Songs emanate from life and they must always depict life. Songs divorced from life are of no significance. Particularly in operatic portrayal, one is liable to lean towards music and neglect the depiction of life. That is why attention must be paid to describing life delicately and richly. The more delicately and richly an opera depicts life, the more deeply and the more broadly it can portray the characters' psychological world and the stronger impression it can make on the audience.

A delicate and rich depiction of life is also needed to give dramatic tension to the storyline. Such a depiction can portray the characters' personalities and events in sharp contrast and from various angles, exposing contradictions more clearly and, accordingly, making the story dramatic. Since a varied and rich life is a prerequisite for a dramatic and interesting storyline, the writer must always strive to depict life in all its delicacy and depth in line with the development of the drama.

A delicate and rich depiction of life is also important in describing historical backgrounds truthfully. Various aspects of life portrayed in all its delicacy and in all its richness can provide vivid and realistic historical backgrounds in all fields of politics, the economy, culture and morality.

The revolutionary opera *The Sea of Blood* describes the historical background of the 1930s truthfully because the portrayal of the life of the heroine's family is not confined to the bounds of family affairs but covers a broad field of politics, the economy, the military and culture, while exposing the true nature of society at that time. It is precisely because this opera describes life in this way that it convincingly proves the truth of the revolution that no force can check the might of the people who have risen up in the struggle under the banner of independence. The aim of such a depiction of life is, in the

28

long run, to give the people a correct understanding of life and show them the way to lead a worthwhile life. Therefore, life which is described in an opera must always contain important human affairs and embody a beautiful, noble and progressive ideal.

In order to describe life in all its delicacy and in all its richness it must be portrayed in detail. This means that life is fully explored in various aspects and described delicately. Life comprises political, economic and cultural activities. Various aspects of life corresponding to the dramatic situation and moments should be explored from various angles and depicted delicately; only then can the opera give people a correct picture of life. If life is shown without details, it is possible neither to represent it in its concrete richness, nor to make the characters animated and provide a broad picture of the historical background and social system.

In portraying the details of life, the actions of characters and the situation surrounding them must interrelate properly. Since an opera depicts life through the characters' actions on the stage, the situation and actions must not be represented separately. In theatrical art, the actions of the characters must always fit in with the situation. This means that in opera the situation should not be explained ahead of the actions, nor should actions that do not accord with the situation be depicted. Dramatic interest is not aroused by the results of the events or actions, but by the life that leads to the results and by the clarification of the characters' destiny in the process of life. If the situation is explained ahead of the actions, the drama showing the characters' destiny will be revealed too early, and the characters' actions related to the situation will naturally be explanatory. If the characters' actions take place out of context, the life depicting the characters' personalities will not be convincing and the development of the drama will creak, with the result that, ultimately, the whole representation will be unrealistic.

In order to write a libretto that conforms with the characteristics of opera, every means of operatic portrayal must be used in such a way that it fully performs its function and role. Writing a libretto in this manner is an important guarantee for improving the ideological and artistic qualities of the opera. Song, speech and dance are important means of operatic portrayal. The writer must compose a libretto which, by means of songs, the basic means of operatic portrayal, depicts the personalities of the hero and other characters and develops the seed in depth. To this end, he must determine the exact content and form of the songs in each scene as well as the way in which the songs can be connected from scene to scene in keeping with the development of the drama.

When composing songs for a libretto, the characters' emotions must be built up carefully while the basis of the life that produces the songs is laid so that the built-up emotions burst out in song in accordance with the logic of the personality and the dramatic situation. If the drama is set with songs monotonously and if the libretto is written in the manner of simply connecting one song to another, then it can be nothing more than a type of variety performance of some solos, vocal ensembles and choruses.

In an opera the songs must be the main element and, at the same time, speeches and dances must be used where necessary. A few spoken words rather than a song can make some scenes realistic, and communicate the meaning more clearly than a song; in some scenes a dance rather than a song or a speech will show the life emotionally and make the dramatic sequence natural. Art can impress the people only when it depicts life truthfully. In a libretto everything must be calculated properly from the beginning and the drama be woven in accordance with the characters' personalities and the logic of life.

A libretto must be perfect from the literary point of view. Only such a libretto can lead the work of the composer and other members of the creative group in the right direction and firmly guarantee the ideological and artistic qualities of the opera. In a libretto the lyrics of songs must be poetic, the speeches meaningful and the words that describe the time and place of the events and the situation and behaviour of characters depictive.

2) LYRICS MUST BE POETIC

The lyrics, as the ideological and artistic basis of songs, are a factor determining the ideological content and artistic value of an opera.

In opera, songs are the means of portrayal which directly expresses the characters' thoughts and feelings in detail, describes life and develops the drama. The lyrics are the main element of a song. Songs dealing with the same subject can be good or bad, depending on their lyrics.

Excellent lyrics are a prerequisite for excellent music. Excellent lyrics are those which induce one to deep thought when listening to them, and which become a song when recited because of their profound meaning and fine portrayal. Lyrics should be meaningful, plain and rhythmical so that they can easily be set to music.

Lyrics must be profound in their ideological content.

It is only when the lyrics have deep ideological content that the story of the opera can be unfolded impressively and the characters' spiritual world be elucidated profoundly. The lyrics of opera songs must contain what the characters think and feel in their mutual relations and what they see, hear and feel in the course of their lives. The librettist can only write lyrics with profound meaning when he explores the characters' inmost world revealed in their mutual relations and in the course of their lives. The lyrics must never contain feelings of characters that are simple or what can be understood clearly from their actions.

The lyrics of opera songs may vary with the requirements of the seed, the characters' personalities and the situation in the scenes; but in general they must represent man's aspirations and desire for an independent and creative life, his strong will to achieve it, his hopes, optimism and other significant elements, all on a high poetic level.

Highly poetic portrayal is the main requirement for lyrics. Such portrayal is the librettist's original discovery based on his passion for life and his philosophical contemplation of the period and human beings. A highly poetic portrayal can only be created when a profound idea is portrayed with warm passion and rich emotion. Noble thoughts and rich feelings are prerequisites for raising the standard of poetic portrayal of lyrics.

Opera lyrics must contain profound philosophy that elucidates the character and essence of the period and inspires people to deep thought. A production can be philosophical when its subject matter, through profound artistic portrayal, induces people to meditate upon the period and life for a long time. In order to create a philosophical image, it is imperative to select a new and original seed and explore the aspect of life which reflects a pressing question of the period, an issue which is vital to the political integrity of the popular masses who make history as masters of the world. Selecting a new, valuable seed, however, is only the first step towards guaranteeing the philosophical depth of a work. No matter how valuable a seed is in the hands of the librettist, he cannot create a philosophical image unless he develops the seed onto a high artistic level through a sincere study of life and deep thought. The philosophical character of a production emanates from the depth of highly suggestive portrayal. Even a single expression in an opera song must have deep meaning and even a single line of a poem should have broad ideological content; only then can the poetic portrayal be excellent and the philosophical depth be ensured.

The song in the night scene in the revolutionary opera *The Flower Girl* is excellent because the lyric has great philosophical depth. The words to the effect that, although there is one moon in the sky, different people gaze up at it with different feelings according to their social status poetically express the contradictions of the exploitative society. As you can see, lyrics can touch the people's heartstrings only when they are philosophically poetic.

Since poetry is a genre of literature which lyrically describes the impact of life and thoughts and feelings from a person's own experience, it is important in making lyrics poetic so that they express the subject matter with rich emotions. A poem expresses thoughts through emotions; so, if it lacks emotions, the thoughts expressed will be crude. A poem rich in emotions can inspire the audience with the thoughts it expresses.

Lyrics which are not poetic lack lyricism and descriptive force. This is the case with songs in general, and the lyrics of opera songs in particular, which are based on specific situations and definite aspects of life, cannot impress the audience if they lack lyricism and are unable to inspire the audience to thought, or if they explain the content of scenes or reveal it directly. Direct expression and crude lyrics in opera songs are a fiasco. Such lyrics cannot serve as the basis of beautiful melodies.

The text of a song must be rhythmic and lyrical. If it is composed of spoken words or of lines of prosaic sentences cut into stanzaic form, it cannot evoke a response from the audience. If the text of an opera song is to be rhythmic and lyrical, it must be composed of set-form verses as required by the stanzaic song. This can deepen the ideological content of the opera and raise the level of its poetic portrayal as well as the artistic quality of the song. A text in rhythmic verse can be set closely to music. A text in free verse is difficult to set to music, and even when it is set to music the song will not be smooth and easy to sing.

In conventional operas the melodies of songs fluctuate violently and are complicated because the texts of the songs are in the style of free verse or of narrative speech, as required by arias and recitatives. Since stanzaic songs require poetic texts that become songs naturally, even if only chanted, all the lyrics of opera songs must be written in stanzaic form.

In order to compose the text of a song in a stanzaic form, lyrics that take the form of narrative speech must be eliminated. Lyrics in this style are a remnant of the recitative opera. It is impossible to create a highly poetic portrayal or a smooth and simple rhythmic flow from this style of text. All the texts of songs, including those for villainous characters, to say nothing of the hero's songs, must be written in rhyming verse; only then can all the opera songs be stanzaic and a highly artistic portrayal be created.

In order to eliminate narrative speech from operas, it is necessary to choose a kernel of dialogue which expresses the characters' personalities, ideas and emotions in everyday life and to write the lyrics in a poetic form. If the lyrics are a jumble of various things, with no essence representing the characters' personalities, ideas and emotions, the texts will

34

lack a keynote and will be unable to express the ideological and emotional content of the production profoundly. The librettist must give a poetic form to the essence of the ideas and emotions flowing out from the experience of the principal and other characters.

Song texts must be comprehensible to the popular masses.

If you are to write comprehensible song texts you must express the characters' ideas and emotions in a simple and realistic manner. Only those song texts which are comprehensible to the people and cater to their tastes can be welcomed by them. They will be excellent songs that are easy to sing. Such song texts not only are comprehensible to everybody but also invite him to chant and sing them.

In order to write comprehensible song texts you must also avoid the use of words of Chinese origin and puzzling words and choose, polish and use words used widely by our people. One simple song text in the revolutionary opera *The Sea of Blood*, to the effect that you may break a bush clover branch with ease, but you cannot break a giant tree, and that women, all united, have the strength to defeat any enemy, clarifies the truth of unity and struggle in plain words. The words of opera songs must be succinct and simple and, at the same time, meaningful.

You must not use vulgar and dull expressions and empty, lengthy phrases simply because you have to write song texts that are comprehensible to everybody.

Although a song text is the smallest form of literature, writing it is not easy. It must be simple in structure, but it must be rich in emotions and deep in the idea it contains. In order to write excellent texts, librettists must acquire deep experience of a diverse, rich life and think at all times. Only when they explore life will new, significant poetic ideas flash into their minds so that they can write excellent song texts.

3) ADAPTATION REQUIRES THE PROPER ESTABLISHMENT OF A PLOT

Adapting to various genres works of art and literature which are widely known and loved by the people for their cognitive and educational value and excellent portrayal is very important in increasing the cultural wealth of the nation.

Artists and writers must, in addition to creating new works, select works of high ideological and artistic qualities from among novels, films and dramas and adapt them skilfully to various other genres.

Adaptation is a new form of creative work. Adaptation translates the ideological content of one original work into another in conformity with the characteristics of the latter form of art and literature. It requires the re-interpretation of a work in accordance with the characteristic of another form of art and literature on the principle of retaining the ideological content of the original. As the manner of depiction and the means of portrayal of the different forms of art and literature differ from one another, their methods of establishing and developing the plot are not the same. The film has its peculiar manner of depiction and means of portrayal, and the same is the case with the opera. Therefore, when adapting a certain work of art and literature into an opera, it should be reshaped to accord with the characteristics of opera.

The plot of an opera has to be established in the translation of a production of one form of art and literature into an opera.

Establishing the plot in adaptation into an opera means reshaping the composition and plot to suit the characteristics of opera. In adapting a film, for instance, into an opera, the dramatic organization characteristic of films must be dissolved, the human relations and events must be re-established to accord with the characteristics of the opera, and the structure and plot must be revamped.

It is most important in adaptation to have a correct understanding of the seed of the original and to preserve it to suit the characteristics of the genre to which it is being adapted.

A work is adapted into another form because the seed of the original is good. So, if its seed is misunderstood or misrepresented, the purpose of adaptation is not achieved. There are some instances in which more emphasis has been given to translating a few scenes in which the portrayal is interesting than to understanding and preserving the seed of the original production, or in which the characters, events and life in the original have been copied without modification. This is not the way to establish the plot in adaptation, nor will such adaptations acquire any significance.

In order to establish the plot in adaptation, primary attention must be paid to the work of analysing and understanding the seed of the original production. Only when the seed of the original work is understood correctly can the structure of an opera be composed on the basis of it to conform with the characteristic of opera, and can the events and details of life be enlarged or omitted in a creative fashion. It was possible to depict the scene in the street at night where the heroine is accused of theft and the moonlit scene where she returns home with medicine in a fresher manner in the revolutionary opera *The Flower Girl* than in the film of the same name because the film was adapted excellently to accord with operatic characteristics on the principle of preserving the seed of the original on the basis of a correct understanding of it.

In order to establish the plot in adaptation properly the structure must be composed with skill.

In adaptation not only must the individual characters, events and scenes of the original be dealt with properly but also the main content must be depicted well in a new structural form. The composition of an opera is different from that of a novel or of a film. Because of the limitations of the stage, an opera requires a concise and intensive dramatic representation of the characters, events and life. *Sea of Blood*-style operas, unlike the operas of the past, can show life in three dimensions through the continuous flow of many scenes, but they cannot describe man and life as a film or a novel can. In making a novel or a film into an opera, the characters, events and scenes of the original must be re-arranged more succinctly to suit the conditions of the stage so as, on the basis of this, to form a new structure.

If you are to compose the structure of an adapted opera properly, you must establish a new plot to accord with the characteristics of opera. If you remain within the framework of the storyline of the original, you cannot establish a proper plot in your adaptation. Nor must you reverse the human relations of the original and the organization of events or leave out important scenes and essential details of life on the pretext of giving life to the characteristics of opera.

The structure must be composed by adapting to the characteristics of the new work the events and characters that exert a direct influence on depicting the seed of the original rather than changing them or discarding them indiscriminately.

In order to establish the plot of the adaptation to the opera, the method and means of portrayal must suit the characteristics of opera.

An opera also differs from a novel, a drama or a film in the method and means of portrayal. The events which have been portrayed in a film through the characters' speeches, actions and other cinematic means are described in an opera by songs, orchestra and theatrical means. This does not mean that the characters' speeches and actions in a film can be put into the characters' songs and actions in the opera as they are. The events which have been described by the characters' speeches in a film can be depicted by a song or by actions, or be omitted, in an opera. Portraying events which have been described by cinematic methods by new operatic methods is a characteristic of adaptation to the opera. As you see occasionally in the course of creation, some emotional scenes in the original work leave no impression in the adaptation, whereas some commonplace scenes in the original are impressive and meaningful in the adaptation. All this depends upon whether or not the plot of the adapted work is established so as to create an original image.

In order to create new images in the adapted work, important scenes from the original must be reorganized to conform with the features of opera. Those scenes from the original which do not promise a good effect must be boldly discarded if discarding them does not hinder the development of the seed, and new aspects of life must be discovered on the basis of the original so that the scenes can be restructured. Even those scenes which have not been given serious attention in the original can be reconsidered and given prominence when necessary to suit the features of opera. In adaptation, among scenes from the original work those which can be omitted or shortened must be boldly omitted or shortened and those which can be developed broadly must be developed in that way so that the scenes which are impressive in the original are portrayed in such a way that they have the same effect in the opera. You must neither omit impressive scenes from the original without fully exploring various ways of preserving them simply because they do not seem to meet the requirement of the stage and substitute them with good songs, nor bring the impressive scenes of the original into your opera intact on the ground that they have to be retained. Even impressive scenes from the original must be reproduced to suit the logic of opera and the depictive features of the stage.

In adaptation, two tendencies must always be guarded against. One is to stage everything of the original work mechanically on the pretext of respecting the original and the other is to depart from the seed of the original on the pretext of recreating it. Copying the original work without re-establishing the plot to accord with the characteristics of the opera is not creation; portraying images at will by departing from the seed of the original conflicts with the nature of adaptation.

Fresh representation through adaptation requires artistic fiction. Even when fiction can be used, the principle of preserving the seed of the original must be observed. Artistic fiction has nothing in common with arbitrary change or the fabrication of life, a departure from the principle of creating typical images. Fiction which is not based on the original and which does not help the preservation of the seed of the original has no significance, although it may seem excellent in itself. Artistic fiction is only significant when it depicts an important aspect of life that can contribute to the development of the original.

The creator's originality must be sustained in adaptation.

Adaptation is not technical and practical work simply to translate a work into another form but a creative endeavour that requires originality. Originality in this work can ensure a more life-like and impressive portrayal of the seed of the original. When creating the operatic version of a novel or a film, the form of the structure, the way of developing the storyline and the style of the portrayal of the original must not be mechanically copied; the ideological content of the original must be translated properly to accord with the characteristics of opera by displaying originality.

With a correct viewpoint and attitude towards adaptation, creative workers must always blaze a path of adaptation.

3. OPERA MUSIC

1) THE STANZAIC SONG IS THE MAIN MEANS OF OPERATIC PORTRAYAL

Songs form the major component of opera. Opera is an art describing people's thoughts and feelings and their lives and weaving drama with song. An opera song should be composed in such a way as to describe the characters' personalities and their lives realistically and represent their thoughts in depth.

(1) Opera Songs Must Be Stanzaic

It is very important to make good use of songs because they are the main means of operatic portrayal. For opera to become a true art for the people, its songs must be composed in a stanzaic form which is liked by them.

A stanzaic song is a song with a text in rhymed verse which is divided into stanzas set to the same melody.

The stanzaic song is the major form of folk music created and refined by the people. It is the major means of operatic portrayal.

Stanzaic songs are easy for the people to understand and sing, and they are familiar to them. Although falling under the category of folk music, the narrative folk song is not much liked by the people because its text has quite a few prosaic elements and its melody sounds like a tuned speech, whereas the stanzaic folk song is enjoyed by everyone because its text is in the form of rhymed verse and its melody is beautiful and gentle. The stanzaic folk song has been sung by the people widely for many years.

In spite of its concise form, the stanzaic song is very expressive and diverse in its descriptive function. The stanzaic song, with its concise text and melody, can express people's inmost worlds emotionally, depict life in a descriptive way and weave human relations dramatically. It can reveal the people's various thoughts and emotions and their complicated psychological worlds lyrically and delicately and describe nature and the various emotional colours of human life vividly. It can also depict the flow of the times, momentous historical events and the people's magnificent advance in great depth and breadth.

The stanzaic song is a powerful means of describing life dramatically. An opera must have drama expressed in song as well as songs expressed in drama. If the drama does not contain songs or if the songs do not flow with the drama, the drama and song cannot be in harmony. The drama must go with the songs and the songs must be sung in the drama. Only then can the drama and music be in unity. In conventional operas the aria has played the major role in expressing the principal character's emotions, and the recitative has played the role of connecting the events and weaving the drama. Such being the case, when an aria was being sung by the hero the flow of the drama slowed down or was interrupted, and when a recitative was being sung the musical character weakened; thus it was difficult to achieve the organic unity of music and drama.

The stanzaic song provides an easy solution to the

problem of coordinating the music and drama in an opera. The stanzaic song facilitates the unity of music and drama because the intercourse and interchange of thoughts and feelings between characters is done by means of songs lines of which are sung by turns by different singers, as is done with work songs. The stanzaic song can also express the characters' inmost depths without obstructing or interrupting the flow of the drama because it can accommodate rich content in a succinct form. When realizing the intercourse and inter-change of thoughts and feelings between characters, the stanzaic song, unlike the recitative, makes the intended idea poetic and sets it to a beautiful and gentle melody; so it can always contribute to the development of the drama without weakening the musical character. The stanzaic song is characterized by its potential to realize the intercourse and interchange of thoughts and feelings between characters and to promote the drama powerfully by means of perfect and refined music.

In order to describe the opera's seed and theme in depth as well as the inmost depths of the characters delicately, and to develop the drama powerfully, the stanzaic song must be made the basis of opera music and the principal means of portrayal, and all songs must be in a stanzaic form.

Making all songs stanzaic is a fundamental principle in the creation of opera.

The art of opera has a history of hundreds of years. However, there has never been an opera in which all its songs were stanzaic. At one time stanzaic songs were used in Western opera, but they were only a small part of the whole of the musical composition, in which the aria was predominant. It could not be said that opera songs had been made stanzaic when the musical form of the aria was preserved while a few arias had been replaced with stanzaic songs. In Western operas the aria has been considered the "flower of opera" that is capable of describing the hero's spiritual world better than any other musical form and which enables the composer and singer to display their musical talents to the full. In this context, more and more complicated and intricate arias have been produced whether the people understand them or not. In some operas free singing parts were included at the close of arias, which gave the singer the "freedom" to perform whatever feats he could. The songs of such operas were so difficult to understand, so unnatural to the ear and so difficult to sing that the people did not like them. The popular masses accept only music that is pleasant to hear and easy to sing; if music is difficult to understand and to sing, they do not accept it, no matter how excellent it is. Many operas have been produced, but most of the songs in them have only been sung on the stage and by a few music fans. They have not become popular because such music as arias and recitatives are not readily accepted by the people.

When *Sea of Blood*-style operas were being created in our country for the first time, some creative workers doubted whether they could indeed create an opera in the musical form of stanzaic songs to touch the heartstrings of the people. That was because they did not regard the stanzaic song as a noble form of music and were reluctant to adopt it. Holding the stanzaic song in contempt is an expression of a bourgeois aesthetic view. The introduction of stanzaic songs into opera music is a revolution in this field.

In order to make opera music stanzaic, the aria and recitative, which have been the main elements of conventional opera, must all be replaced with stanzaic songs, both the songs of the characters and the *pangchang*. In addition, orchestral music must be arranged and played in a variety of forms and by a variety of methods to suit the characteristics of

45

stanzaic songs. For the transformation of opera music into stanzaic songs it is also necessary to sustain the characteristics of stanzaic songs in the musical communication between characters. In the early days of creating *Sea of Blood*-style operas some creative workers, because they had an incorrect understanding of the introduction of stanzaic songs, made each character sing a new song whenever he appeared on the stage. Even when characters with common thoughts, feelings and aspirations interacted and intercommunicated on the stage they were made to sing separate songs. If stanzaic songs are introduced into opera in this manner, all the songs in an opera will be similar, drab and tedious. Doing this is an outdated technique of musical dramaturgy. Characters in the same position and with the same aspirations should be made to sing one song which accords with the thoughts and aspirations of each character, to sing lines with different words in the same song, by turns, rather than sing different songs. One stanzaic song with lines with different words which express intercommunication between characters will be clear in its content, easy to understand and familiar to the audience.

It is important to compose musical masterpieces for stanzaic songs in operas.

The aim of introducing the stanzaic songs into opera is to produce musical masterpieces that are intelligible and enjoyable to everyone. Even an opera with stanzaic songs cannot impress the people unless its songs are excellent. Only when an opera overflows with excellent music can its stanzaic songs prove their worth.

A musical masterpiece is a song which the more one listens to it, the better it sounds, which the more one thinks over it, the more profound its meaning becomes and which the more one sings it, the more one wants to sing it. In other words, it is a song which contains life and profound thoughts and is rich in emotion; it is a song with a gentle and beautiful melody, a song which the more we hear it, the better it sounds and which the more we sing it, the more we want to sing it.

A good song always inspires the people with confidence and courage and encourages them to a new struggle. The revolutionary songs of the period of the anti-Japanese revolutionary struggle, the songs of the days immediately after liberation, the songs of the years of the Fatherland Liberation War and many songs of the period of postwar reconstruction and of socialist construction served as a powerful weapon for encouraging the popular masses to perform great feats of heroism. Composers must compose every single song to inspire the people dynamically to the revolution, masterpieces that can be sung not only today and tomorrow but also in the distant future.

It is not easy to compose such a song. A song which seems to sound good when it is heard at first but is not appealing after being heard several times is not an excellent song.

In order to compose excellent songs the composer must explore people's lives and experience their noble moral world in depth. Art represents life. A truthful portrayal of life is a genuine work of art and literature. A noble and beautiful melody is found in life. The composer must discover melodic images and bring his musical conception to maturity in the course of experiencing people's lives deeply.

The composer must penetrate not only people's lives but also the world of his own work. The heroes of our operas are prototypes of the times who embody a noble moral world and sublime moral traits. The composer who creates an opera must penetrate the world of his work so as to understand the hero's thoughts and feelings correctly, and he must discover a melody that can portray the hero's ideological and moral qualities accurately and in depth.

(2) Melodies Peculiar to a Nation Are the Basis of Opera Music

In order to make opera songs stanzaic and fill the opera to overflowing with excellent songs, good music must be composed. An excellent song plays a major role in giving the people a correct understanding of life and in encouraging them forcefully to the struggle to create a happier and more worthwhile life. Every single song that is composed must be polished artistically so as to be an excellent song in which high ideological content is expressed naturally through noble artistic qualities, a song which touches the heartstrings of everyone.

Music must be composed on the basis of our nation's own melodies.

Composing music on the basis of these melodies is a policy our Party has been maintaining consistently in the development of socialist national music. The ideological and artistic qualities, the popular character and the national character of music are determined by the melodies on which they are based.

Our music must become art that reflects our people's lives, their thoughts and feelings and serves the Korean revolution—Juche art. If it is to reflect our people's lives and emotions accurately, opera music must be composed on the basis of national melodies that have been created by our people and refined over a long period of time.

Creating opera music based on our national melodies is a principle in creating our national opera. By national melodies

48

I mean those which represent the sentiments that are peculiar to a particular nation. A nation has its peculiar sentiments that have been formed historically and artistic forms that are suitable for expressing them. The Korean people like songs and dances which are elegant and gentle and drawing which is light and clear. Our opera music must be created to accord with these national sentiments of ours.

Folk songs are representative of music with national melodies. Folk songs have been composed to reflect the people's thoughts and feelings formed in the course of labour and life and, as such, are rich in national characteristics. During their struggle to harness nature, transform society and defend the land, our people have created many gentle and beautiful folk songs and enjoyed singing them, while refining them continually. Folk songs reflect people's feelings and sentiments in detail.

The melodies of Korean folk songs are clear and soft without steep changes in their pitches, and they are gentle and beautiful. Folk songs based on such melodies are succinct, clear and easy to understand and sing. These songs have been liked and sung by our people for many years not only because they reflect their own feelings and desires but also because their forms are easy to understand and sing.

Although folk songs are representative music that is based upon national melodies, some of them do not cater to the modern tastes of our people. Folk songs were produced and developed in the class society, so they have socio-historical and class limitations. From the point of view of the working class and modernity, we must preserve those folk song melodies which accord with the aesthetic tastes of our people today and discard those which do not.

Retaining folk song melodies that are not liked by the people of our times is a tendency to return to the past. Such a tendency in the creation of art and literature would beautify the exploitative society and the life of the exploiting class, glorify outmoded and antiquated things and, consequently, distort or debase the noble national character of our people. At present, the reactionary bourgeois theoreticians of art and literature and the artists of south Korea are, on the pretext of sticking to the national character of art, reviving the court music, court dance and the like that served the feudal rulers. They are presenting the *pansori* that the feudal noblemen enjoyed singing, as if it were representative of the musical heritage of our nation. Some of them even allege that dancing, and singing in a hoarse voice, with a topknot and horsehair hat on the head and with a traditional robe flying is national art. This, in essence, is ignominious behaviour that distorts our sublime national art and debases our nation as an uncivilized nation. On no account must we tolerate even the slightest tendency that debases our nation, distorts our national art and tries to return our modern art to the past.

National melodies are not immutable. The outdated and stale elements among the national melodies are eliminated with the development of the times, and the beautiful and progressive elements are refined, and thus the treasure-house of national music is enriched. National melodies are enriched not only by new folk songs of the new age but also by excellent songs composed by professionals. Excellent songs composed by professionals become folk songs over the course of many years, and their melodies and tones are added to the stock of national melodies. In our country there are not only folk songs that have been sung from time immemorial but also the progressive folk songs that were composed in the 1920s, the revolutionary songs which were composed and spread widely during the anti-Japanese revolutionary struggle and the popular songs composed after liberation. These songs have their own distinct national melodies as well as traces of having overcome the limitations of the national melodies of the past. Our folk songs of the past are soft and lyrical; some of them, however, lack vivacity. Many of the new popular songs created on the basis of folk music are soft, lyrical and lively. The fine melodies of popular songs have taken their place firmly in the music of our country by being gradually established as melodies peculiar to our nation. Over many years the melodic elements that are outdated and do not conform with the people's aspirations have been discarded, and new melodic elements, the product of the new age and new life, have been added. Thus our national melodies have been developed and enriched constantly. This, precisely, is the law-governed process of the development of national melodies. Therefore, national melodies must not be identified with those of folk songs but be understood in a broader sense.

The characteristics of national melodies are clearly expressed in their tones. The tone is the basis and the smallest unit of a melody, but even so it embodies national feelings and timbre. People can guess whether a melody is Korean or not simply by listening to its tone, because it embodies national characteristics.

Composers must, as a matter of course, study our revolutionary songs, folk songs and popular songs closely and discover among them Korean tones and melodies which suit our people's national feelings and tastes and use them widely in musical creation.

Sea of Blood-style operas overflow with national feelings because the folk and other songs which were created and widespread in the past have been incorporated in them in conformity with the characteristics of opera music, and the tones of these songs were preserved in every way. Drawing on the valuable experience gained in creating *Sea of Blood*-style operas, composers must produce all opera music on the basis of our national melodies and in accordance with our people's tastes and sentiments. Our people do not like a mixture that is neither Korean nor Western music. Only songs with rich national melodies are accepted, loved and sung joyfully by our people.

Making the melodies of songs gentle and beautiful is one of the principles of creating music for *Sea of Blood*-style operas. Doing so is an essential requirement in composing stanzaic songs.

A gentle melody means a natural melodic flow emanating from the impact of the lyrics of a song.

It is only when the melody of a song is gentle that the meaning of the words can be understood and the people can listen to it at ease and appreciate the deep meaning of the song with composure.

In musical composition, creating gentle melodies and setting them in due order must not be confused. By a gentle melody I do not mean only orderly melodic development. The orderly development of a melody is an aspect of making it gentle, but all the notes cannot be arranged in order. If a melody ascends and descends in a gentle curve all the time, the song will be too monotonous to the ear. It is not our way to make the melody ascend and descend excessively, over-whelmed with emotions provoked by the lyrics of the song. In order to make the melody gentle and beautiful, the notes must be arranged in a natural manner in accordance with the situation of the drama and the inmost world of the principal character, as well as with the meaning contained in the lyrics of the song and its emotional colour.

If gentle and beautiful melodies are to be composed, the dramatism of the song must also be understood correctly.

An opera song is the song of a character who is in a

dramatic relationship, so it must be dramatic. Songs without dramatism cannot be opera songs. The melody itself must not be made artificially dramatic simply because opera songs have to be dramatic. Since dramatism can underlie gentle songs, you will be perfectly able to sustain the dramatism if you organize the drama skilfully. The songs *I Shall Remain Singleheartedly Loyal* and *Do Not Cry, My Dear Ul Nam* from the revolutionary opera *The Sea of Blood* have gentle and beautiful melodies, but they are strongly dramatic because the meanings of their words harmonize with the situation in the scenes in which they are sung. In particular, the song *Avenge the "Punitive Expedition"* leads the people into the world of the drama with strong dramatism because not only is the melody of the song good but also its words are deep in meaning. That is why, when producing the revolutionary opera *The Flower Girl,* gentle and beautiful melodies were composed first to accord with the idea and emotion of the lyrics, and then they were made dramatic at subsequent stages of portrayal.

Temperate and beautiful melodic composition must not result in feeble and slow melodies. Composing temperate and beautiful melodies is one thing and producing feeble and slow ones is another. A song's melody must be vigorous and carry weight while being moderate; it must be lively and fresh while being elegant. A lifeless and spiritless song cannot inspire strength and courage in people. Although its melody is temperate, the song *The Snow Falls* is vigorous and carries weight; the song *My Happy Country* is moderate and simple, although its melody is lively. A song whose melody is gentle and yet vigorous, graceful and yet full of vigour, is precisely a song of our style.

It is important to make good use of Korean tunes in creating opera music on the basis of national melodies.

The tune expresses feelings peculiar to a nation. The music of a nation has its own tunes.

Our national music has a rich variety of tunes. Our forefathers have given wonderful musical expression to their noble feelings by means of tunes that suit our national music.

In order to preserve distinct national characteristics in musical composition, the composer must make effective use of the unique timbre of our folk melodies and the rich variety of Korean tunes.

If he is well-versed in Korean tunes, he can compose a song which is better suited to our people's tastes and emotions, although the melody may be in the same tempo and key. A song which is composed with a distinctive tune that is properly suited to the content of its lyrics can express national feelings well.

In the composition of opera music the lyrics of a song and its melody must be set precisely to each other.

Matching the words and music well is a principle that must be observed in the creation of songs.

A close alliance between them means artistic harmony. In a song the tone of the melody is based on the tone of speech. The tone of speech finds tangible expression in the attitude of the speaker, the pitch of his voice, its tune, stress and timbre. Likewise, the tone of the melody varies according to changes in the people's thoughts and emotions. Therefore, to discover a temperate and beautiful melody, a close study must be conducted into the characteristics of the tone of our language.

Needless to say, tones of speech and melody are not identical. Although it is based on the tone of speech, the tone of a melody is still more distinctive, more regular and more measured than that of speech in its pitch, tune and stress. Therefore, the tone of a melody requires polished, poetic words. The melodies of folk songs are always allied with rhymed verse. This explains why the words of songs must be stanzaic and poetic in order to produce national melodies.

In order to obtain a good alliance between the words and melody of a song, it is necessary to make the best use of the good points of the Korean language in setting music to the words so that the melody follows the poetic rhythm in a natural way. Only when the poetic rhythm and the tone of the melody weld into a harmonious alliance will an excellent piece of music be produced.

For a good alliance between the words and music, the tones of the melody must be arranged to suit the syllables of the words. If not, the meaning of the lyrics will be distorted, or the flow of the melody will be unnatural.

(3) Opera Songs Must Be Idiomatic

Even if all the opera songs are stanzaic, the stanzaic composition will be meaningless unless the songs are idiomatic.

The aim of introducing stanzaic songs into opera is to weave the drama with novel and idiomatic songs which the people can understand easily and enjoy singing.

It is only when opera songs have their own characteristics that they can mirror the individual features of the characters and those of life realistically and attract the interest of the audience. People see operas in order to enjoy good songs. If all the songs in an opera are composed in the same manner people will not go to see the opera. The songs of an opera must be idiomatic and fresh from the beginning; then the audience will wait for the songs in the following scene with interest and expectation and will be drawn into the drama in spite of themselves. Composing idiomatic songs is, in the long run, a factor in raising the ideological and artistic qualities of the opera and strengthening its cognitive and educational functions.

In order to compose idiomatic songs for an opera, set patterns and imitation must be avoided.

Some operas contain similar songs. Some songs are alike not only in their melodies but also in the lines of their texts. The tendency to imitation is revealed notably in copying pieces recognized as good. Needless to say, a close study must be made of the good aspects of a song for emulation if its lyrics or melody are recognized as good. However, emulating such a work after a close study and copying it mechanically have nothing in common. In creation, stereotype and imitation hinder the development of freshness and variety in art and literature.

Stereotype and imitation in creative work result from the lack of an original spirit of inquiry and creative enthusiasm. Imitation emanates from a spiritual void and absence of experience of life and artistic talent. Imitation and plagiarism bring disgrace on creative workers. An artist who, with a highly creative spirit, loves people and life and is well-versed in art, never imitates others. Bearing in mind that stereotype and imitation in creative work result in disaster, creative workers must combat them. Composers must understand the essence of life from the creative standpoint and with an original attitude so as to compose fresh and idiomatic songs.

In order to compose idiomatic songs for an opera, their timbre must be distinct.

The timbre of opera songs must accord with the personality of the characters.

The characters appearing in the opera all have their own tasks of portrayal. Even a secondary character plays a role that no one else can do in expounding the seed and theme of the opera; so the songs of each character have their own tasks of portrayal. The timbre peculiar to these songs does not come of its own accord simply because every song has its own task of portrayal.

When creating the revolutionary opera *The Sea of Blood,* it was considered that the original song in the scene in which the guerrilla operative meets the mother, the heroine, and persuades her to work for the revolution posed no problem in carrying out its portrayal task because its text was good and the melody was smooth. But it had no artistic appeal for the listners because of the absence of emotional timbre peculiar to the song. That was because the composer paid attention only to the technical aspects of the task of depiction without exploring the political operative's thoughts and emotions on meeting for the first time the mother who, bereaved of her husband, was gradually being awakened to revolutionary consciousness while undergoing every manner of hardship. Even a song whose portrayal task is clear cannot have emotional appeal unless the composer produces timbre appropriate to the song.

The timbre of an opera song gives musical expression to the emotions emanating from the characters' personalities and the dramatic situation. If the composer is concerned only with superficial phenomena, instead of penetrating the inmost thoughts and feelings of the character, he will have difficulty in catching the emotional timbre emanating from the character. A song, however skilfully composed, cannot be good if it lacks emotional timbre derived from the personality of the character.

The emotions involved in the dramatic situation must be represented in a lifelike manner if idiomatic songs are to be composed. Since opera songs are sung by the characters in a specific situation, the songs must express the emotional

57

atmosphere of the situation as well as the emotional state of the characters. Only a song which corresponds with the characters' experience and the atmosphere of the situation can be a lifelike, idiomatic song for an opera.

In creating an opera some songs, which have been included in scenes as a result of their apparent profound meaning and emotions, have to be omitted because the emotional content of the songs does not suit the dramatic situation. In an opera a song which does not correspond with the situation must be dropped without hesitation and a new song composed to replace it.

Opera songs must have their own characteristics, and yet maintain internal connections according to the characters' personalities and the logic of the dramatic development. They must form a harmonious unity as integrated opera music.

Opera songs must be composed in such a way that they harmonize with one another. Only then can the characteristics of musical portrayal be preserved and its unity be realized. Harmony without characteristics is meaningless, and musical timbre which lacks harmony cannot produce the desired effect. Even if the songs are idiomatic and correspond with the personality and situation, the general musical image will be lacking consistency, and the dramatic sequence will seem broken unless the songs are in harmony. On the other hand, if the timbre of the theme song is copied in other songs for the sake of the harmony of the overall musical image, all the songs will resemble one another and will sound dull to the ear. Composers must never seek harmony for harmony's sake. Harmony for its own sake cannot give life to the timbre of songs; it will even end in destroying the harmony. Harmony is always achieved through the contrast and combination of characteristic elements, so the timbre of the songs must not be sacrificed for the sake of harmony. Instead, the musical timbre must be clear for the sake of harmony. Distinct musical timbre and its harmonious unity are essential for the creation of excellent opera music.

An idiomatic melody is the product of original thinking, inquiry and passion. The creator's standpoint and attitude, as well as his passion, are reflected directly in his creation. His creation shows his ideological level and the scope of his heart. Just as a factory worker says "If you want to know my thoughts, look at my products," so a creative worker must say "If you want to know my thoughts, look at my creations." With such an attitude you will be able to compose excellent songs. You can never create novel and colourful songs with illusions and skilful fingertips on a keyboard. Composers must always penetrate man and life and experience them in real earnest; they must sing from the bottom of their hearts with warm passion. Profound thought and the spirit of inquiry with which to choose one piece from a hundred pieces they have composed, as well as tireless creative passion and originality and audacity to blaze the musical trail that nobody has trodden will enable them to compose fresh, idiomatic masterpieces that will be sung down through the generations. The more such songs there are, the more deeply the opera will find its way into the people's lives.

2) THE *PANGCHANG* IS SOMETHING OF OUR OWN STYLE

One of the essential characteristics of *Sea of Blood*-style operas is the introduction of the *pangchang*. The *pangchang* in opera is something completely of our own style, and it is new and original.

(1) No Aspect of Life Is beyond the Descriptive Power of the *Pangchang*

The *pangchang* is a song that, off the stage, describes the world of the drama. It is a new musical means of portrayal that is capable not only of descriptive delineation beyond the reach of stage songs but also of dramatic or lyrical portrayal.

In former days only the characters' songs and orchestral music were considered to be musical means of portrayal in opera. This was because the operas of the past were based on the long-established theory of the opera. This theory only recognized lyrical portrayal directly expressing the characters' thoughts and emotions and dramatic representation expressing the characters' relations by means of song and action, on the ground that the opera was also a form of dramatic art; it never recognized lyrical portrayal dealing with life from the point of view of a third person. Therefore, in the operas of the past all the songs were sung only on the stage and the characters' personalities and life, and the dramatic relations among them were portrayed only through their songs and orchestral music.

The operas produced in our country in the 1950s and the early 1960s were not free of this framework. The opera *Tell O Forest* created in those days is the moving story of a guerrilla political operative who, working as a village headman in the enemy area during the anti-Japanese revolutionary struggle, rouses the people to the struggle for national liberation. This opera had great significance in that it was the first to deal with our revolutionary traditions, but it failed to solve quite a few descriptive problems. Choe Byong Hun, the hero, is a revolutionary who fights, overcoming all his mental suffering, being held in every manner of contempt and disdain by the villagers because he has to work in the guise of the village headman. He keeps the secret of his identity even from his daughter and, at the crucial moment, lures the enemy to destruction at Hongsan Valley, where he dies. The creative workers intended to stir strong emotions in the people through the death of the hero Choe Byong Hun, but, contrary to their subjective intention, the audience felt empty. Rather than thinking that the hero died a worthwhile death the audience felt forlorn at his death because he died without seeing the bright world for which he had worked so arduously underground. The death of a fighter who devoted all his life to the revolution must not give people a forlorn feeling. The hero should have survived to see the reward of his struggle and victory.

The opera *Tell O Forest* also had problems with its musical interpretation. In that opera even the vocatives, to say nothing of such words of action as "come", "sit down" and "go", were set to music in the form of the recitative, so they were awkward to the ear. Worse still the hero, at the moment of his death, was made to sing an aria expressing his thoughts. For a dying man to sing in an opera does not accord with either the logic of life or the logic of portrayal.

Opera is an art which represents life mainly through music, but there should be no rule that all aspects of life must be described in stage songs. In the opera speech can be employed when the actions of a character can be more appropriately portrayed in speech than in song. When it is awkward for the character himself to express his own feelings, a third person can express his thoughts in song off the stage. It is an outmoded way of thinking to insist that in an opera life must, without exception, be knitted by music and that the character himself must sing his own thoughts, whatever the

61

circumstances. As life is rich, so the manner of its portrayal must be varied.

Realism is the lifeblood of art. The conventional methods of portrayal which hamper the realistic depiction of life must be altered to meet the requirements of the period and the aspirations of the popular masses, as well as to accord with the nature of art. This is precisely the Juche creative attitude. There is no need to portray life exclusively by means of stage songs, sticking to the outmoded pattern.

Having studied the operas of Korea and various other countries, we realized that it was impossible to portray the moral traits and life of our contemporaries perfectly through the conventional form of opera consisting of stage songs and orchestral music. We reaffirmed our decision to conduct a revolution in opera. We introduced the *pangchang*, a completely new means of musical interpretation, into *Sea of Blood*-style operas.

The introduction of the *pangchang* in opera, along with that of stanzaic songs, is a particularly important success in the opera revolution.

The introduction of the *pangchang* is significant in that it has enabled the new style of opera to depict man and his life in a natural and realistic way.

The *pangchang* not only describes the situation but also shows the inmost thoughts and feelings of the characters from different angles, represents the period and life in great breadth, adds great momentum to the drama and links the stage and the audience. The *pangchang* is a powerful means of portrayal that can represent every dynamic aspect of life and any subtle shade of psychology. The introduction of the *pangchang* has furnished the potential to show from various angles and in greater depth and breadth the hidden aspects of the life of characters and their inmost selves, which are beyond the descriptive power of stage songs, and to give a life-like musical interpretation to the seed and theme of a work.

The significance of the introduction of the *pangchang* lies in the creation of a new style of opera capable of describing different aspects of life in depth by means of songs being sung in turn on and off the stage to suit the dramatic situation and development.

By the introduction of the *pangchang*, a third form of music, into opera, which previously consisted of stage songs and orchestral music, a new opera music consisting of stage songs, orchestral music and *pangchang* has been evolved. This makes it possible to enhance the descriptive function of stanzaic songs and to enrich the musical portrayal beyond measure through a proper combination of stage songs and *pangchang*, *pangchang* and orchestral music, and *pangchang* and *pangchang*, and through their contrast and harmony. The employment of the *pangchang* has brought about a radical change in opera. It is a revolution that has opened up a new realm in the style of opera and musical dramaturgy.

The *pangchang* holds a very important place in opera and plays a major role in it.

The *pangchang* is a powerful means to portray the inmost thoughts and feelings of a character in an opera in great depth and breadth from various angles.

In opera stage songs directly express the inmost thoughts and feelings of the characters; but these songs cannot describe the characters objectively, so the characters experience certain limitations in revealing their inmost selves. The *pangchang* can describe the characters freely from both the objective and the subjective angles, describing their inmost world in breadth and depth.

The *pangchang* furnishes the potential to portray the characters' inmost depths particularly from the objective

63

point of view.

The *pangchang*, from the objective viewpoint, mainly supports the characters' actions and describes their thoughts and emotions from the point of view of the creative artist. In the revolutionary opera *The Sea of Blood* the scene in which the mother learns to read and write shows how deeply the *pangchang* can portray the heroine from the objective viewpoint. The *pangchang*, *The Mother Learns How to Read and Write,* describes the mother sitting on the earthen floor at the front of the room, burning the midnight oil to learn to read and write from her youngest son and warmly sings of the heroine's noble mind reflected in her action. If that scene had been portrayed by means of songs sung alternately by the mother and son in the manner that was used before, it would not have created such a strong impression on people. In this scene the mother and the son do not sing but hold a dialogue of a few words and perform some actions, and the *pangchang*, together with the orchestra, unfolds the depths of their lives and the mother's pure mind, so that everyone who sees it cannot but be moved.

The *pangchang* can also describe the depths of the characters' minds objectively in scenes of illusions or dreams. Of course, orchestral music can also do this. But it is difficult for an orchestra to express so clearly the characters' aspirations and wishes reflected in illusions or dreams as distinct linguistic images do. In such scenes the *pangchang*, employed along with orchestral music, can produce a clear image of a character's imagination and dream and add variety to the portrayal in a scene. The *pangchang* can also revive impressive events in characters' past lives and unfold their hopes for a beautiful future.

The *pangchang* can also depict in strong relief the inmost thoughts and feelings of a character. In other words, it can

64

play the role of a mouthpiece which expresses something that the character himself is not in a position to express or a state of mind that cannot be described by anything other than monologue. In dramatic art it is very important to depict an event which cannot be represented by the character himself, as well as the hidden aspects of his life. In life there are circumstances in which one cannot express one's own feelings or finds it more natural to have someone else speak for one. In the operas of the past the principal character himself was made to sing even in such cases. As a result the character often found it difficult to express his anxiety properly or he described his life in an awkward manner. In a drama such situations can frequently be dealt with through a monologue or narrative, but these methods are not appropriate for an opera. A situation that can be expressed through a narrative in a drama must be portrayed through a *pangchang* in an opera. It is only when the *pangchang* speaks for the character and shows even the hidden aspects of his life, which are difficult for him to speak about, that the personality of the character can be more realistic and the scope of the opera music widened. Musical interpretation by the *pangchang* reveals a character's inmost thoughts and feelings alternately with the character's songs. The better the *pangchang* performs this function, the more naturally the audience is drawn into the world of the drama, accepting the experience of the principal character as their own.

Although it is an off-stage song, the *pangchang* has great power to emphasize the characters' personalities and to depict their inmost thoughts and feelings delicately. In opera, therefore, the *pangchang* is no less important than the principal character's song. In all cases it can show the characters' ideological and spiritual worlds if they are difficult for them to depict or cannot be shown by means of stage songs or the orchestra.

The *pangchang* is also a powerful means of deriding or denouncing negative characters from an objective standpoint. In the operas of the past their villainous nature was described either through their own songs or recitatives or through their actions, or they were exposed and denounced through the form of a chorus by the positive characters. These methods cannot easily reveal their villainous nature clearly. In some operas many scenes were clumsy because, while a positive character denounced the negative character face to face by means of a song, the latter waited silently until the singing was over and then acted as if to say "what?". In such scenes the *pangchang* must satirize or condemn a villainous character's action from an objective standpoint, or the heroic character's standpoint. Thus it can expose the villainous nature more clearly and describe the characters' actions on the stage realistically.

The *pangchang* is a powerful means of broadly outlining the period and society as they relate to the hero's destiny; thus it makes an active contribution to describing their essential nature in full. It is also an instrument with which the creative worker can make an aesthetic appraisal of the event taking place on the stage. Art can accurately describe the law of historical development only when it provides people with a realistic portrayal of the essence of the period and society. To do this, life must be depicted in depth from various angles and the experience gained by people in the course of their lives explored delicately. The more broadly and deeply a character's life and his inmost thoughts and feelings are described, the more the essential nature of the period and society will be clarified.

In exposing the essential nature of the period and society the class character of the society of the period, if it is not yet understood by the principal character, can be described from the point of view of the author, as is done through the *pangchang When Did the Toilers Appear in the World* in the scene in the revolutionary opera *The Flower Girl* in which Ggot Bun goes to the landlord's as his servant. The true nature of the exploitative society, which is full of contradictions, can also be exposed from the standpoint of the audience and of Ggot Bun and her sister, as is done by means of the *pangchang Faith Moves Mountains* in the scene of her mother's death, through the outpouring of hatred for and curses on the cruel, exploitative society which tramples mercilessly upon the pure hearts that are devoted to their mother and orphans them. The *pangchang* exposing the true nature of the period and society in the context of the life described on the stage is similar to the narrative description of a novel which outlines the period and society broadly and provides an in-depth philosophical interpretation of their true nature.

The *pangchang* provides the opera singer with conditions for realistic acting. In an opera, the singers must sing while acting realistically and act realistically while singing. Only then can they create true-to-life characters. In the operas of the past it was an iron rule that the characters' personalities should be represented only by means of stage songs and orchestral music. The singer had to sing all the time and was scarcely able to act. Such being the case, many songs were songs for song's sake in the operas of the past, and the singer found himself tied to the songs, hardly able to create images through acting. In conventional operas the personalities of the characters were abstract, their acting was clumsy and the flow of the drama was tedious because the singers were forced to sing unnaturally and their acting was neglected. The *pangchang* provides the characters with satisfactory conditions for free action while describing their inmost thoughts and feelings and explaining the situation and environment of the drama from the standpoint of a third person and while singing their thoughts from their standpoint. As a result, the characters have become able to act realistically and animate the opera stage with the help of the *pangchang*.

The *pangchang* is a powerful means of developing the drama.

The main means of expressing dramatic development in former operas was the recitative and orchestra. Although arias and the characters' acting influenced the dramatic development, they did not play a significant role. The *pangchang*, free from such limitations, works actively on the development of the drama. In an opera the *pangchang* promotes the development of the drama alternately with the songs sung on stage by the characters. If the *pangchang* is given excessive emphasis in disregard of the dramatic situation, or if it alternates with the stage songs at any moment simply because it is a musical form that has a strong influence on the dramatic progress, then it may have an adverse effect on it. Therefore, the stage songs and *pangchang* must be introduced when appropriate after the dramatic situation has been carefully examined.

The *pangchang* also promotes the development of the drama independently, according to the dramatic situation. The *pangchangs* in the scene of the mother's death in the revolutionary opera *The Flower Girl* and in the scene in which convalescing Myong Ho practises walking in the revolutionary opera *A True Daughter of the Party*, give great momentum to the drama in harmony with the characters' acting, but without any emotional echo of their songs. The appeal of these *pangchangs* comes not from the objective description of the characters' actions but from the psychological depiction of their inmost thoughts and feelings. The stage only shows the main characters' actions, but the *pangchangs* express their emotions in depth in support of their actions so as to give a strong impetus to the drama and impress the audience.

In an opera the drama can be connected and developed by employing *pangchangs* between scenes and acts. If the *pangchang* is introduced along with orchestral music as the stage slowly darkens, an emotional connection with the following scene can be achieved naturally and the drama be developed smoothly while particular emotions are evoked as the stage moves. If the *pangchang* is used when connecting the scenes in a work that covers a long historical period, the passage of time and the changes in life can be described naturally without any particular explanation or change of stage. It would be a good idea to provide a lingering effect by means of the *pangchang* along with orchestral music if necessary when the curtain is lowered.

The *pangchang* is a powerful means of effecting emotional communication between characters and the audience and of linking the stage and the audience.

Making the audience believe the events depicted on the stage to be true and accept the characters' ideas and emotions as their own while laughing and crying with them—this is the power of realistic stage art. In former operas the characters responded to one another mainly by reciprocating songs, so there were some limitations to realizing a rapport between the characters and the audience. In *Sea of Blood*-style operas the *pangchang* links the stage and the audience to provide emotional communication between them, sometimes depicting the mind of the character and sometimes expressing the minds of the audience, thus helping the stage and the audience to breathe the same air.

By conveying the feelings of the characters to the audience, the *pangchang* plays the role of a bridge between the stage and audience. Listening to the *pangchang*, the audience actively responds to the appeal of the character and sympathizes with him and follows his actions.

Moreover, the *pangchang* conveys to the character what the audience wants to tell him, so it draws the audience into the drama. The *pangchang* *Let Our Girl Soldier Slumber Gently and Deep* in the revolutionary opera *A True Daughter of the Party* is sung after the heroine falls asleep with a spoon in her hand as she watches the wounded soldiers delightedly eating the meal she has prepared with the rice she has obtained from an occupied village at the risk of her life. Representing not only the minds of the wounded soldiers who, with warm camaraderie, want to see the girl soldier sleep just for a moment but also the minds of the audience who is observing her beautiful deeds, the song says: "Birds of the forest, do not chirp now! Let our girl soldier slumber gently and deep." In the earnest *pangchang*, the audience's warm feelings towards the heroine are conveyed to the stage and the audience is impressed by her beautiful spirit so that the audience and the stage experience the same feeling.

As you can see, the *pangchang* holds a very important place and plays a significant role in improving the ideological and artistic value of an opera and freshening its quality.

(2) The Greater the Variety of the *Pangchang* Is the Better

The *pangchang* is a good means of portrayal, but it can only be effective when it is used where it is needed; it can only prove its worth when it is used properly. Creative workers must make the best use of the *pangchang* and improve our style of opera.

The *pangchang* must be used in accordance with its characteristics. It can be sung independently or in unison with or alternately with the stage songs, or it can depict the psychology of the principal character. In all cases, however, it is sung from an objective point of view. It is characterized by its effectiveness in describing the depths of life beyond the reach of the stage songs, always from an objective point of view. When producing an opera, the creative workers must seriously consider which scene is appropriate for an objective representation of man and life and must employ the *pangchang* in such a scene. It must also be used in scenes in which it is difficult or impossible to express the characters' inmost thoughts and feelings by means of stage songs alone. Only when the *pangchang* is used where it is needed can its descriptive function be enhanced and its peculiar timbre be maintained.

The *pangchang* must be used in a variety of ways to suit the scenes. The stage always reveals new aspects of life. In the course of constant change and development in life with new events taking place in succession from the first scene to the last, the characters' personalities develop and the theme of the work is clarified. Life that changes and develops without interruption requires a variety of new songs. No piece of music can take the place of the *pangchang* in describing various aspects of life. Since it can describe various aspects of life in great depth and breadth from an objective point of view, from a third person's standpoint, there can be no end of variety in the operatic portrayal of life if the *pangchang* is used in appropriate scenes.

The *pangchang* must be used in conformity with the personalities of the characters and the situations in the drama.

What is important in this regard is to employ it on the principle of sustaining the stage songs. This is because it has the descriptive task of emphasizing and giving life to the stage songs. In an opera the personalities of the characters and the dramatic situations are portrayed in detail by means of stage songs. No matter how effective it is, the *pangchang* cannot produce good results apart from its emotional communication with the stage songs. Even its independent employment can be significant only in the context of the stage songs in the previous and following scenes.

In an opera a song sung by the principal character is the most important of the stage songs. Only when a song by the hero is sustained is it possible to describe his personality accurately and clarify the seed of the opera properly. The *pangchang* plays a major role in sustaining songs sung by the hero. Needless to say, other characters' songs, too, support the songs of the hero and emphasize his personality, but they are not so effective as the *pangchang*.

There are several methods of using the *pangchang* to support the songs of the hero and emphasize his personality. In harmony with the hero's song, the *pangchang* strengthens the emotion. The principal character in an opera usually sings the theme song or major songs. These songs are the best and most refined of opera songs. More often than not, however, even a good song, if sung on its own, sounds rather simple. It would be a good idea for an opera singer to sing a melodious song alone and also in harmony with a *pangchang* when necessary. If the *pangchang* backs up a vocal solo in various ways, it can produce peculiar emotional colours that cannot be produced by a solo alone and arouse people's emotions more delicately in a harmonious way. But, for all that, the *pangchang* must not be stressed at the expense of the solo. The solo on its own has great depictive significance. When the

72

hero's song is joined by a *pangchang,* the solo must be protected well and backed up in such a way that it penetrates the *pangchang;* it must not be repressed or hindered.

The *pangchang* must be used in a well-harmonized way not only with a song by the hero but also with other characters' songs, which must not be neglected on the ground that they are songs by secondary characters. Even though they are songs by secondary characters, if the *pangchang* represents the characters' ideas and emotions or stresses their personalities, enriching their songs in an objective way, their characterization can be so much more vivid.

Another important factor in using the *pangchang* to suit the personalities of the characters and the dramatic situation is that it must be used in various forms according to the growth of the characters' personalities and the development of the events. In the course of creating *Sea of Blood*-style operas various types of *pangchang,* such as a solo *pangchang,* duet *pangchang,* small *pangchang,* medium-sized *pangchang* and grand *pangchang* have been evolved and various methods of using them to conform with the characteristics of the opera have been developed.

Creative workers must skilfully use the various types of *pangchang* and the methods of portrayal which have been created in *Sea of Blood*-style operas to conform with the personalities of the characters and the dramatic situation. In an opera, even the same song requires different musical interpretations depending on the forms, for instance, a small *pangchang* or grand *pangchang;* the *pangchang* also produces a variety of emotional climates in a scene depending on the timbre, for instance, a women's *pangchang* and men's *pangchang.* The musical interpretation also differs depending on the sequence of the characters' songs and the *pangchang.* In short, ten types of *pangchang* and ten methods of interpretation are required for ten different situations. Choosing the type of *pangchang* is not simply a technical and practical matter but creative work to sustain the characteristics of the *pangchang,* to realize the general harmony of the musical interpretation of the opera and to raise the level of its ideological and artistic qualities. Creative workers must employ every single item of the *pangchang* with care.

What is important in dealing with the *pangchang* so that it conforms with the characters' personalities and the dramatic situation is to use it in a proper combination with the grand ensemble. The grand ensemble, as a new form of opera vocal music evolved in *Sea of Blood*-style operas, is the biggest form of chorus involving all the positive characters on the stage and all the members of the *pangchang* group. It is mostly used when the dramatic relations reach a climax or when they are settled. The *pangchang* must powerfully develop the drama in harmony with the stage songs and then, in a scene in which the dramatic emotions reach a climax or in which they come to a head, it must join the grand ensemble.

The *pangchang* must be used well, in harmony with the dances and orchestral music.

Stressing the ideological and emotional content of dances is essential in combining the *pangchang* with them. As in the scene of the Mt. Paekdu dance in the revolutionary opera *The Sea of Blood,* a wordless *pangchang* can be included initially, culminating gradually in a grand *pangchang* singing of the indomitable spirit of our people who are fighting staunchly, looking up at the noble image of Mt. Paekdu. As in the scene of a dance in a dream in the revolutionary opera *The Flower Girl,* the *pangchang* in different forms can sing either of the heroine's past life or of her beautiful hopes for the future, following the line of her destiny and emotions. On particular occasions, such as in the scene in which a dance is performed by a symbolic method, a wordless *pangchang* can breathe life into the dance and give it peculiar appeal.

It is also important to intensify the emotional colour of the dances and sustain the dance movements. In order to create an emotional impression on the audience, the dance must be performed to beautiful and temperate music. When the *pangchang* matches the dances, it plays the role of not only emphasizing the content but also accompaniment, sustaining the dance rhythms.

The *pangchang* must also harmonize with the orchestral music. In harmony with the orchestral music, it can, by describing the inmost thoughts and feelings of the characters realistically, explain aspects of the plot that cannot be described by orchestral music and thus play the role of linking the orchestra with the stage songs and fulfil the function of connecting different scenes. The *pangchang* which accompanies orchestral music must be used in various ways to accord with the resonance and timbre of the orchestra. When it is accompanied by an orchestra which connects different scenes the music of the orchestra must be gradually replaced by that of the *pangchang* so as to produce a long, lingering effect.

A variety of methods of connecting one *pangchang* with another must also be explored.

While maintaining harmony with the stage songs, dances and orchestral music, the *pangchang* must always preserve its peculiar timbre. Variety in the employment of the *pangchang* with its own timbre to suit the dramatic situation and context is the key to enriching the characterization and musical interpretation of opera.

3) WHEN THE ORCHESTRAL MUSIC IS ALIVE, THE STAGE IS ALIVE

In opera, orchestral music plays the important role of increasing the effect of the songs, of welding the drama into one musical flow and of integrating the stage representation into a harmonious whole. Songs are the major elements of opera, but whether they are effective or not depends largely on the role of orchestral music. It is only when orchestral music supports the songs well, sustaining their main melodies, that the musical interpretation will be profound. No matter how good a song is, it cannot prove its worth if it is not well-supported by orchestral music.

In opera orchestral music fuses the characters' songs, the *pangchang* and all the other songs into one musical sequence. Opera songs, no matter how many and how excellent they are, may sound like a mere collection of songs unless they form one stream. In an opera the orchestra is the only means of drawing songs into one stream and ensuring the consistency of the music. Playing continuously throughout the development of the drama, the orchestra connects one song to the next, supports the characters' speeches and actions, strengthens the rhythms of the dances in harmony with them and allows the stage movement to flow; it links the stage movement into one musical flow and realizes the unity of the image.

Playing independently in an opera, it also emphasizes the characters' personalities, develops the drama and broadens the opera's musical interpretation. The effect, dramatic progress and animation and ardour of opera songs on the stage depend on how the orchestra is used. Bearing in mind the role of orchestral music in an opera, the creative workers must work hard to create and develop an opera orchestra of our own style from our own standpoint.

(1) Orchestral Music Must Be Based on Stanzaic Songs

Orchestral music in our opera must be popular, national and modern.

If opera is to be an art to serve the people, the orchestral music of the conventional opera, which is difficult and complicated, must be discarded and a new one which appeals to the feelings and aesthetic tastes of the people created. The correct way of creating new orchestral music for opera is to develop it on the basis of stanzaic songs.

From the point of view of musical development this is the age of stanzaic song. Our people today require stanzaic songs that have been created and refined by the popular masses. Regarding this trend as "simplicity" is the way of thinking of the exploiting class who despise the people. It is the aesthetic view of the bourgeoisie. It is the popular masses who create and enjoy true art. The art loved by the masses is the noblest and truest of arts. At the same time as introducing stanzaic songs into opera, we must develop new orchestral music for opera of our own style which is based on these songs.

This means that, as an accompaniment to opera songs, orchestral music should sustain these songs on the basis of their stanzaic melodies and that, in independent performance, it should not only follow the stanzaic melodies but also modify and amplify them by various methods so as to effect symphonic portrayal.

This principle must not mislead you into trying to

reproduce the stanzaic melodies. Basing orchestral music on stanzaic melodies does not in the least mean reproducing these melodies. Such a reproduction is mere accompaniment, not orchestral music.

The new orchestral music for opera is incomparably superior to the conventional one not only in describing the theme of the opera and the personalities and lives of its characters but also in achieving unity of portrayal with the vocal music and developing the drama.

As a direct accompaniment to stage songs and the *pangchang* the new opera orchestra enhances the songs' power of expression by emphasizing the meaning of the songs and the melodic emotions through the orchestral tone, and adds to the emotional depth of the characters' personalities and lives. Even when being performed independently, the new orchestral music modifies and amplifies the melodies and the tones of the stanzaic songs by various techniques, effecting symphonic depiction, so that it sounds more familiar to the audience, attracting them to the world of the drama with ease, than the conventional one which developed the music by means of the so-called leitmotiv and flexible melody lines.

The new opera orchestra is also superior to the conventional orchestra in ensuring the consistency of the music. In opera, orchestral music and songs must not be fragmentary, nor should the orchestral timbre depart from the general mood of the music. An opera must begin with music and end with music; life should unfold with music, and the drama should develop with music. All songs and orchestral music must contrast with one another and yet harmonize with one another so as to become welded into one mood. In new operas, musical integration can be achieved easily because the orchestral music is based on the theme melody and on the principal melodies derived from the theme melody not only when accompanying the songs but also when supporting the characters' words and actions and interpreting dramatic situations and dances.

The new orchestral music of opera, which is based on stanzaic songs, is the best one in that it promotes the songs' artistic qualities and their dramatic functions and enriches the musical interpretation beyond measure. It is popular orchestral music because it sounds familiar to the audience.

Creative workers must firmly maintain our own standpoint and produce and develop orchestral music of our own style which is capable of an impressive portrayal of characters' personalities and lives, and of making the stage resound.

(2) Orchestral Music Must Be Alive

When the orchestral music is alive, the stage is alive. By lively orchestral music I mean a variety of orchestral resonance that, in harmony with the situation, gives life to the inmost feelings of the characters, animates the atmosphere in the scenes and develops the drama powerfully, breathing the same air with the stage.

In order to make the stage alive, the orchestra must skilfully perform the functions of both accompaniment and musical drama. When it accompanies a song, it must keep the song alive; when it is played independently, it must give a strong impetus to the dramatic development while fusing the song and the dramatic flow.

The orchestra must accompany songs skilfully.

Accompaniment is a form of performance to support the musical interpretation of songs by means of orchestral resonance. Skilful accompaniment is very important in enhancing the ideological and artistic qualities of opera and in raising the level of musical interpretation of songs. The standard of a song's musical interpretation depends upon the level of the orchestral accompaniment. The accompaniment must be subordinated to giving life to songs. It must lead the songs so that they start naturally; when the singing has begun, it must support it well and cover it softly; and when the singing has come to an end, it must wind it up properly so as to leave a lingering effect.

The accompaniment must always be played on the principle of preserving the principal melody of the song. An accompaniment that does not keep the principal melody alive not only blurs the ideological and emotional content of the song but also lowers the level of its interpretation. It must sustain the timbre of the principal melody and lead the singer to sing with ease; it must help the listeners to be drawn spontaneously into the world of the music.

In opera the orchestral accompaniment sustains the dramatic character of the songs. All opera songs are sung at certain moments of the dramatic development, so they assume dramatism. In order to bring the personalities of the characters to life and describe dramatic situations by means of accompaniments to songs, the dramatism of songs must be sustained by orchestral techniques. The songs sung in the scene of the amusement quarters in the revolutionary opera *The Flower Girl*, where Ggot Bun is branded as a "thief", and in the scene of crossing the River Namchon in the revolutionary opera *A True Daughter of the Party*, are strongly dramatic. When accompanying such songs, the orchestral music cannot emphasize the meanings of the songs and the dramatic emotions merely by covering and supporting them. When dealing with such songs, the accompaniment must go beyond the range of the general concept of accompaniment and strengthen the dramatic character of these songs. In other words, variety and alterations must be provided according to their character and mood. Only then can the accompaniment emphasize the ideological content of the songs, penetrate the inmost thoughts and feelings of the characters, bring the emotional atmosphere of the situation to life and give life to the stage.

The orchestra must fulfil the function of providing dramatic music. Orchestral music for opera differs from ordinary accompaniment in that it interprets life by emphasizing characters' personalities independently as required by the dramatic development, and adds momentum to the dramatic development. A piece of music that does not fulfil this function satisfactorily cannot be called orchestral music for opera.

If orchestral music is to fulfil the function of dramatic music, you must penetrate the world of music, the world of orchestral music. This means that you should conduct intensive creative research into ensuring a skilful orchestral interpretation of the psychology of the characters and their dramatic emotions that are difficult to express in songs and dances. By nature, orchestral art is art that shows a person's inmost nature through the harmonious resonance of various instruments. Its fascination is that by this means it can portray man's inmost depths that cannot be expressed through spoken or written words, as well as the noble, beautiful, romantic and heroic elements of human life, in a peculiar way. In opera these expressive capabilities of orchestral music must be employed to the full so as to portray the inmost thoughts and feelings of the characters in a deep and subtle way; then both the orchestra and the stage will be alive.

In order to make the orchestral music fulfil the function of dramatic music properly, music that connects songs must be

81

used skilfully. The skilful employment of it allows for a consistent musical sequence and the unity of musical interpretations, as well as the natural singing of singers.

Music that connects songs and develops them must integrate the songs that are sung in different situations. Because they are sung at different stages of the dramatic development, opera songs must be joined into one flow by the orchestral music and assisted and led to act strongly on the dramatic development. To perform this function, orchestral music should be arranged in a way different from the manner of arranging ordinary songs. What is important here is to eliminate the tendency to use stereotyped preludes, interludes and postludes in every song. If this tendency is tolerated, opera music will sound like a mere collection of songs. Worse still, it will be impossible to provide the natural connection of characters' emotions and impart tension to the dramatic sequence. Music that connects different songs and develops them must always be dealt with by a variety of techniques to suit the characteristics of the songs and the situation in the scene, as well as the logic of life and the dramatic development.

While covering gaps during the characters' speeches and actions on the stage, interludes must penetrate the depth of the opera music and link the dramatic action and music organically. In an opera the characters must speak, act and dance always in the context of the music. Their speeches and actions can only be impressive and meaningful in the context of the music. An uninterrupted flow of orchestral music enables the characters to act naturally in tune with the musical flow. If music is not provided, the speed of acting of the characters may vary; but if music is provided, they can act steadily and realistically because they act to the accompaniment. In a scene where the characters merely act and speak, without singing, orchestral music must concentrate on portraying the characters' inmost thoughts and feelings and maintaining the emotional atmosphere of the situation rather than on describing the actions and events superficially. Only orchestral music that follows the emotional flow can portray the world of music vividly and in great breadth.

In order to employ connecting music to suit the characters' inmost thoughts and feelings and the emotional atmosphere of the situation, orchestral music must skilfully provoke the characters' feelings to continue towards and reach the climax in a natural manner and leave a long, lingering effect. While giving a hint of the new songs and new scenes to come, it must also create an atmosphere for fresh interpretation. Only then can the drama enlarge the world of the music indefinitely and develop along the emotional line exuberantly.

For the orchestra to fulfil its function of performing dramatic music, it must provide a high standard of musical interpretation of the scenes. The scenes hold a very important place in an opera. Each scene in an opera involves stage songs, the *pangchang,* the characters' speeches and actions, and dances. It is the main task of orchestral music to fuse all these artistic elements into a single emotion and effect a consistent musical flow. A scene which includes orchestral music is precisely where the orchestra should resound by displaying its artistic skill to the fullest. In a scene which includes orchestral music, the orchestra must emphasize an in-depth interpretation of the characters' ideas, emotions and psychology. Here the orchestra must, by various methods of portrayal, make the best use of not only the theme song and other major songs but also their derivative melodies, so as to create an integral, symphonic resonance. To this end, the stanzaic songs' melodies must be prolonged and broadened freely and boldly as the situation and atmosphere demand so that the orchestra resounds endlessly. By a resounding orchestra, however, I do not mean a superficial representation of events and actions producing roaring sounds. A piece of orchestral music that cannot express the characters' inmost thoughts and feelings will merely sound loud and noisy. It will be meaningless, and appealing to nobody. Even when supporting an event or an action, it must represent in an emotional way the characters' inmost depths that cannot be expressed by actions or words. When it is stirring, dynamically representing the characters' psychology in step with the dramatic development and the situation, the orchestra can have a strong effect on the dramatic representation and great appealing force.

If it is to bring the stage to life, the orchestra must perform its accompaniment to dances skilfully. Just as a good musical piece enlivens a dance, so stirring orchestral music can bring the stage to life. The essence of dance music lies in sustaining the patterns of dance movements. Movement patterns are the lifeblood of dance. Harmonious dance patterns and measures are a must in creating a beautiful dance. What is important in dance music is skilfully to handle that part of the music which starts the dance as well as that which marks the divisions in the dance movements. Nothing is more awkward in dancing than a discrepancy between the moment when the rhythmic movements are started and when the music is started. Only when the music matches the rhythmic movements can the dance be harmonious; and only when the moment is defined clearly by the music can the dancer dance with confidence. Besides, the divisions in the dance movements must be defined distinctly by the dance music. In a dance the movements in the rhythmic flow must be distinct, so the orchestra must support the dance in such a way as to mark the divisions in the movements by means of distinct divisions in the musical flow.

(3) National Instruments Must Be Combined with Western Instruments

Instrumentation is of great significance in enhancing the role of an opera orchestra.

Conventional orchestration is concerned mainly with the combination of Western instruments. Needless to say, the number of instrumental groups is important in that it affects the role of the orchestra. However, from the point of view of developing opera in our own way, it would be a biased attitude to deal with orchestration simply as a matter of deciding the number of instrumental groups. In our country, where both traditional, national instruments and Western instruments are available, the question of the composition of the orchestra must not be confined to a numerical concept. Arguing about the number of Western instrumental groups alone, while ignoring our national instruments, is an expression of a departure from our own standpoint.

In order to develop opera orchestras of our own style we must combine national and Western instruments properly. Each country and each nation has its own characteristic music and instruments as well as those adopted through exchange with other countries. We have fine national music and national instruments that have been evolved over thousands of years, down through history. In our country, where national culture began to flourish a long time ago, musical art was developing and a variety of music using many of our national instruments was being performed magnificently as early as the Middle Ages. Our advanced music has had a great influence on the development of music in other countries. Since the end of the last century, when exchange between East and West became active, Western music and Western instruments were introduced into our country and began to have an effect on the musical life of our people. That was the beginning of the existence of two styles of music in our country. That was an inevitable result of the worldwide exchange in national culture and arts. This historical phenomenon must not be ignored when we develop new socialist, national culture and arts. The point at issue is from which standpoint and with what attitude you consider the mixture of different national cultures, and in which direction and on which principles you develop your national culture. When approaching our national music and Western music, national instruments and Western instruments, we must always maintain our own standpoint and the attitude of considering them with our people at the centre and of making them serve our people. We must neither take to national nihilism by making a fetish of Western music and Western instruments and ignoring our own national music and instruments, nor must we practise national chauvinism in developing our national music by rejecting Western music and instruments indiscriminately.

In order to develop musical art of our own style, we must adhere to the principle of developing it with the main stress on our national music and instruments and subordinating Western music and Western instruments to them. If we depart from this principle we will be unable to develop our musical art properly.

In order to subordinate Western music to our national music and ensure the priority of our national instruments over Western ones, we must hold our national music dear and improve and perfect our national instruments so as to cater to the modern tastes of our· people. We cannot develop our national music and instruments if we look down on them, regarding them as backward and Western music and instruments as modern and superior. In general our national instruments have clear and beautiful timbre and are rich in expressive power, but the sounds of some of them are weak and dull. In the field of music the characteristics and strong points of our national instruments must be used as well as possible and their weak points improved. Unless the weak points of our national instruments are improved, our national music cannot be developed in conformity with modern tastes. If they are to perform the music of any modality successfully, our national instruments must be improved. Forming a modern orchestra with better national instruments is one of the basic methods of subordinating Western music to Korean music and giving priority to our national instruments over Western instruments.

A modern orchestra of our own style has now been formed and it can depict the multifarious aspects of our people's lives and their rich psychology superbly and play opera music on any theme expertly. This orchestra has acquired characteristics that no other orchestra can beat in its scale, its timbre and its methods of performance. It has been developed into a Juche, modern orchestra that can digest any Western instruments. Experience shows that, when national instruments are improved and their characteristics are used as well as possible, the problem of subordinating Western instruments to our national music can be solved.

In order to subordinate Western instruments to Korean music, we must use them properly. Only then can they express our people's emotions and contribute to the singing of our people's life. Subordinating Western instruments to Korean music is a principle in developing our national music, and it meets the aspirations of our people.

There will be no problem even if Korean music is played

on Western instruments. Of course, our musicians may perform world-famous pieces of Western music on Western instruments, and that is natural. Musicians will be able to improve their artistic skill and develop Korean music more rapidly only when they have a good command of Western instruments and are versed in Western music. At one time the symphony orchestra was unpopular with our people because it did not perform much of our national music on Western instruments but a lot of Western music. Therefore, we saw to it that a good symphony orchestra was formed and that it performed Korean folk songs and famous songs that were widely known among our people in a manner congenial to their feelings and tastes. Since then, our symphony orchestra has been loved by our people. This shows that when our musicians perform musical pieces which our people like, even on Western instruments, they can enjoy the people's love and contribute to the development of Korean music. Creative workers must not, in trying to assert our national character, reject Western instruments, but make the best use of the excellent aspects they have.

In order to subordinate Western instruments to Korean music and so contribute to the development of our music, we must combine national and Western instruments properly. A new orchestra must be formed, combining our national and Western instruments on the principle of making the best use of those qualities of the latter which appeal to our people's feelings and of rejecting those which do not. Creating a new composite orchestra of our own style is a pressing requirement for applying the popular character and national characteristics to the art of music and raising the level of its ideological and artistic qualities. Our present situation requires that a variety of new elements of portrayal and forms of expression be created constantly in all fields of art. The elements of artistic portrayal and forms of expression change and develop continually with the passage of time and the development of life. Music, too, can sing of life more broadly and deeply and contribute actively to enriching the treasure-house of human culture only when Korean and Western instruments are combined well.

A Western orchestra combined with our national bamboo-wind instruments with clear and soft timbre was once formed. As such national instruments as bamboo-winds that produce a plaintive but elegant sound and the *changsaenap* that heightens the zest were included in the orchestra, its national characteristics were intensified and the music sounded much better to the ear. A national orchestra which included some special Western instruments was also formed. This resulted in a national orchestra with distinct national characteristics and modern appeal. Needless to say, these were partially combined orchestras. With only a partially combined orchestra the Party's policy on creating a composite orchestra of our own style could not be carried out. Therefore, when effecting an opera revolution, we made sure that an orchestra was formed by a full-scale combination of national instruments and Western instruments. The composite orchestra which has been created in the course of producing *Sea of Blood*-style operas is our own original orchestra which gives firm priority to our national instruments while combining our national instrumental groups with those of Western instruments. By creating the orchestra in which the national and Western instruments are fused on a full scale, we have provided a brilliant solution to the long-standing problem of the co-relation between our national and Western instruments, and our orchestra has become a national, popular and modern orchestra with a peculiar timbre and a great, rich sound that no other orchestra of the past could ever produce. The creation of such an orchestra of our own style is a major success in the opera revolution.

For the proper combination of Korean and Western instruments, we must evolve orchestration in our own style.

To this end, we must implement the principle of properly combining *haegum* (a four-stringed Korean fiddle—Tr.) and bamboo-winds that produce clear and elegant sounds with those Western instruments that suit our national melodies and the characteristics of our beautiful and temperate songs. Particular attention must be given to sustaining the characteristics of our bamboo-winds. The main principle of operatic orchestration is to give prominence to the national timbre of the music and to combine Korean and Western instruments accordingly. Either Korean instruments or Western instruments can, of course, make up the larger proportion as the circumstances require.

For our national instruments to be prominent in the orchestra they must play the leading role. If not, they will be of no significance, however many of them are included in the orchestra. For them to play a leading role, our national instruments must play the leading melody in the principal part. However, it would be impossible for our national instruments to play the leading melody in all cases. Under certain circumstances, Western instruments can play it. In these circumstances, too, national characteristics must be kept alive in the resonance of the orchestra in general, and the combined performance of national and Western instruments must produce a peculiar timbre. If the timbre of Western instruments alone or that of national instruments alone is produced, the composition of a composite orchestra will be pointless. The aim of the full-scale combination of national and Western instruments is, in essence, to evolve a new orchestra congenial to our contemporaries by making the best use of the strong points of the national and Western instruments. Therefore, the national and Western instruments must be arranged correctly and employed according to the content of the work.

In order to sustain national characteristics in the new orchestra, it is necessary to improve and make effective use of the playing techniques peculiar to our national instruments. If they are played in an outdated fashion, the new orchestra, no matter how well combined, will not produce great results. Outmoded techniques should be eliminated from national orchestra and new ones perfected and, at the same time, the techniques of playing Western instruments must be developed in our own manner. In this way the new, popular composite orchestra of our own style will develop and flower to the full.

(4) Musical Arrangement Is Essential

Good musical arrangement is essential to enlivening songs and orchestral music in an opera.

Musical arrangement means making the sound of the original music polyphonic, expanding and transforming it and changing the original instrumentation. It is the creative work of amplifying and deepening the ideological content and emotional tone of the original piece.

It is only when a piece of music is arranged well that the melodic idioms of the orchestra and its emotional tone can be amplified and deepened and a harmonious interpretation realized, and the stage brought to life by rich musical resonance through a skilful performance.

Excellent arrangement in the art of music is no less important than discovering new, melodic idioms. Composers must concentrate their energies on arrangement, regarding it as an important aspect of their creative work.

When arranging a piece of opera music, first of all, the structure must be worked out well.

Arranging opera music is the work of interpreting the theme and thought of the production with stronger emotions by building up contrast and harmony and unifying the whole of the opera music in a single mood while sustaining the idioms of the different songs and the orchestral music. Unlike the arrangement of an ordinary song, the arrangement of opera music can be completed only through complicated processes. It requires solutions to a host of problems—how to arrange all the songs and the orchestral music from the overture to the finale, how to integrate different songs and orchestral music into a single mood, how to organize and play the instruments, and so on. The composer can find satisfactory solutions to these problems only through careful work in structuring all the musical pieces involved, on the basis of his profound understanding of the production. The structural plan of arrangement is what a design is to architecture. As an architect must draw up a good design in order to build a magnificent building, so a composer must frame a musical arrangement to the last detail in order to arrange his opera music excellently. If he becomes absorbed in portraying separate songs or an individual piece of music for a scene without his own original plan for the structure which fits the distinctive features of the work and the character of the music, he cannot produce a good arrangement of opera music. Bearing in mind the significance of framing the structure of the arrangement of opera music, composers must give it definite precedence.

Opera music must be arranged in such a way that it is easy to understand, pleasant to hear and has a national flavour. It is an important principle of musical arrangement to embody popular character and national features.

In order to implement this principle, the ensemble must be dealt with skilfully. An excellent song gives people a strong impression because it contains profound meaning and noble emotions; but these qualities cannot be represented fully by a melody alone. The breadth and depth, the delicate emotional tone and the profound meaning of the melody can find expression only through musical arrangement. It is only when the arrangement matches the sounds of the several parts harmonically that the meaning will be deepened further and the emotional colour heightened.

Harmony in musical arrangement must be handled in such a way that, while using as many harmonized chords as possible, they are not monotonous but interesting. However, this does not mean that compound chords, dissonance and the like must never be used. In order to make a melody powerful and create a deep impression, compound chords or dissonance must be used where necessary. The point in question is how to use compound chords or dissonance effectively to retain the deep meaning of a stanzaic song's melody and intensify its national flavour.

In musical arrangement contrapuntal melodies and changes of key must be used well. These are necessary to sustain the principal melody through various musical sounds; so they must be used accordingly. If, in disregard of this requirement, contrapuntal melodies are used and keys are changed frequently in the musical arrangement, the smooth flow of the principal melody will be hindered and the national flavour will be lost. In particular, it is not our way to use an unnecessary contrapuntal melody on the pretext of using countermelody or to force a singer to produce a loud or long sound in the last part of a song on the pretext of making the song dramatic. Our art must cater to the tastes and emotions of our people. To meet this requirement art must be fully popular. Artistic quality separated from popular character is of no use. When a composer uses a chord or a contrapuntal melody or changes a key, he must do so in such a way that it is understood and accepted easily by anybody, and this he can do by at all times basing himself on the standpoint of serving the people.

Musical arrangement must be original and unique. In an opera each song must be arranged in a unique way; only then can the timbre of the song be sustained and the musical interpretation be idiomatic.

In order to create a new, idiomatic musical interpretation in the arrangement, the composer must think in a creative manner with a correct point of view on musical arrangement and with great enthusiasm. Without thought and passion, he cannot produce an excellent musical arrangement. The composer must always set and pursue high objectives. He can produce a new, original musical arrangement only when he thinks hard, devotes himself totally to his pursuit and burns with creative passion.

In order to produce an original musical arrangement the composer must have his own definite creative opinions and audacity. The composer cannot succeed in arranging a musical piece if he cannot interpret the original work in his own way and conceive an audacious creative plan for portraying it in an idiomatic way. He might fail in the pursuit of a new musical arrangement. Yet the composer who, afraid of failure, deals with a musical arrangement timidly can never produce a brilliant work. The composer must not be afraid of failure but create new portrayals continually.

In musical arrangement the content of the original and the mood of the opera music must not be sacrificed for the sake of originality. In opera musical arrangement is necessary to

94

emphasize the ideological content and emotional colour of the original and unify the modalities of the songs and orchestra. He must, therefore, pay close attention to ensuring the unity of the modalities of the overall opera music while sustaining the characteristics of individual songs. Only the composer who always adopts a fresh approach towards the original and creates new musical interpretations without interruption by means of arrangement can master the art of arrangement.

For the composer to arrange music well, he must be highly skilful. Musical arrangement is a re-creative effort to enrich the meaning of the melody of the original and its timbre, so the composer must know how to use his skill. If a musical piece is arranged in a simple manner, on the pretext of making it easy to understand, the music will become too monotonous to the ear; and if it is arranged in a complicated manner, on the pretext of using skill, it will be impossible to create musical interpretations that suit the tastes and emotions of our people. Composers must know how to arrange music in a fresh manner to suit the tastes and emotions of the people of our times, while making wide use of all the progressive and excellent techniques of interpretation that have been evolved.

4) MAN AND LIFE MUST BE DEPICTED IN SONG

In opera the skilful organization of the musical drama is essential to representing man and his life realistically.

The organization of the musical drama means the method of portraying man and his life dramatically in various musical forms and by various musical means. In other words, it means the method of organizing drama by means of songs and the orchestra.

Opera is the largest form of the musical art comprising various forms of songs and orchestral music. A single opera includes dozens of songs sung by the characters, *pangchang* songs and a variety of orchestral music. But these songs and music, no matter how many and no matter how varied, will be meaningless unless they are fused to clarify the theme of the opera and to describe the characters' personalities and lives. They become powerful means of portrayal only when they are arranged properly to meet dramatic requirements and to accord with the logic of portrayal, and when they form a natural flow of feelings and emotions. Whether an excellent drama is portrayed or not by harmonizing the songs and orchestral music depends entirely on the organization of the musical drama.

(1) There Should Be a Theme Song in an Opera

What is important in the organization of a musical drama is to produce characterization by means of songs and orchestral music. Characterization is only possible when the ideological and emotional depths of the characters are depicted. An opera can depict a man's ideological and emotional depths to the full by means of music, dance, fine arts and acting. The point in question is how to describe the characters' personalities vividly by using the descriptive possibilities of the opera.

The portrayal of the hero is essential in musical characterization. The principal character represents the quintessence of the seed and theme of the work and leads the drama, standing at the centre of events. In works of art and literature the life-like portrayal of the heroes can have a profound artistic effect and enhance the ideological and artistic level of the works.

In the organization of a musical drama the principle of concentrating the songs and orchestral music on giving life to the hero must be maintained. All the songs in an opera have their own parts to play, so their content and emotional tones vary. But they must be subordinated to clarifying the seed of the work and must contribute to the characterization of the hero.

In opera the theme song holds an important place in the characterization of the hero. The theme song plays the pivotal role in bringing out the theme of the opera, giving life to the personality of the hero, developing the drama and unifying the modalities. In other words, it represents the opera music. There are many songs in an opera, but not all of them play a direct part in clarifying the seed. Some of them emphasize the characteristics of the period, some of them describe the situation in scenes and some of them describe the beauty of nature and the change of the seasons. Of all these the theme song embodies the seed of the opera and the characteristic features of the hero most vividly, and plays the pivotal role in developing the drama.

The theme song must be a masterpiece in terms of both words and music. The words of the theme song must portray the theme of the work and the hero's thoughts and emotions deeply in succinct, poetic words; its melody must be fresh and refined and convey the deep meaning of the words of the song. The words and music of the theme song must be deeper in philosophical meaning and more beautiful than those of other songs. They must be perfect. The theme song must have strength to connect the drama and heighten it at every important moment of the opera. Only such a song can provide a realistic description of the hero's mental and moral traits and personality and play a satisfactory pivotal role in the organization of the musical drama.

In opera other major songs must also be well-composed. In opera the personality of the hero cannot be described fully and deeply by the theme song alone. An opera needs, along with the theme song, other major songs that support the theme song. A supporting song is a song which contributes to the portrayal of the personalities of the hero and other major characters and the theme thought, while playing no less an important role than the theme song in developing the lines of the characters and events. An opera contains an entanglement of various characters and events, lines, with the hero at the centre; in the course of the development of these events, the spiritual world of the hero and other characters is clarified, the drama deepened and the theme brought out. The supporting songs, dealing with each of the lines of the characters and events and drawing them into one flow, contribute to revealing the personalities of the hero and other characters and clarifying the theme. The song *Do Not Cry, Ul Nam* in the revolutionary opera *The Sea of Blood* is sung at the moment when the curtain rises and is repeated several times until the scene where Ul Nam falls, hit by an enemy bullet; it also develops the line of warm tenderness between the mother and her son consistently and provides a profound clarification of the process of the formation of the heroine's revolutionary outlook on the world. The song *When Women Are All United,* sung in the scene in which the mother goes to the town on the first mission given her by the revolutionary organization, is repeated in the scene of sending supplies in support of the guerrillas and in the scene of the meeting of the members of the Women's Association at a mining village, showing the growth of the personality of the mother after she has understood the meaning of the revolution and stressing the idea of unity. As you can see, while being sung along the action line of the principal and other major characters and the line of major dramatic events, the supporting songs deepen the theme of the opera, emphasize the personalities of the principal and other major characters from various angles and give strong impetus to the dramatic development. If the theme song is referred to as the pivot of opera music, a supporting song can be called a second or third theme song which plays the role of a beam supporting the pivot. Therefore, in order to portray the personalities of the hero and other characters in song, the supporting songs must be composed well and used effectively.

Impressive use of the hero's initial song is important in characterizing the hero. The hero's initial song describes the features of the period and the circumstances and aspirations of the hero and lays the foundation of the characteristics of his personality. Therefore, the hero's initial song must be impressive and easy to understand.

In order to ensure the prominence of the hero in the opera, the personalities of other characters must be portrayed skilfully in music. A man always lives in social relations. Even the hero who appears in a work of art or literature can display his personality only in the course of mixing with other characters. In a work of art or literature the secondary characters must not be treated lightly on the ground of emphasizing the hero. If the hero alone is made to sing the excellent songs and the other characters only the ordinary songs, the line of the hero cannot be sustained. In opera, satisfactory characterization can be produced only when the inmost depths of both the hero and the other characters are portrayed in full by means of songs and orchestral music.

(2) Music and Drama Must Be Closely Allied

In opera an important task in the organization of the musical drama is to ensure a close alliance between the music and drama.

The ideological content of an opera is developed through the storyline and brought out by the characters' actions. The ideological content of an opera would be inconceivable without them. The storyline of an opera is developed by the songs, not by the characters' speeches, and the characters' actions take place in the midst of songs. Hence, the importance of allying music closely with drama in the creation of opera.

It is not easy in practical creation to synchronize music and drama. In an opera musical pieces cannot last too long in disregard of the dramatic situation for the sake of sustaining the music, nor can a lot of characters' actions and speeches be performed in order to give prominence to the drama. A piece of music, however excellent, cannot be sustained, nor can it give life to the drama, unless it is synchronized with the drama. In conventional operas a close alliance between music and drama was impossible. A satisfactory solution to this problem has been found through the introduction into *Sea of Blood*-style operas of stanzaic song and the *pangchang*.

In order to provide a close unity of opera music and drama it is necessary to find a solution to the problem of combining lyrical and dramatic elements. In *Sea of Blood*-style operas the music can be allied easily with the drama because the characters' personalities and the dramatic situation are described not only in a lyrical manner but also in an epic and dramatic manner on the basis of the stanzaic songs which perform various functions. In addition, their alliance is facilitated by the *pangchang,* which describes the characters' actions and the situation objectively, developing the drama by fulfilling a number of functions which cannot easily be performed by stage songs.

In order to synchronize the music and drama, you must use songs and orchestral music to suit the scenes. The scene is the basic unit of dramatic composition. It is a dramatic phase in which human relations are established, events are developed and the elements of the dramatic development are concentrated. Through the natural sequence from one scene to the next the human relations are deepened and the drama makes steady headway, thus bringing out the characters' personalities and the theme of the work. Only when the scenes are highly dramatic and artistic can the drama develop steadily. Therefore, composers must channel their efforts into portraying each scene in the opera as a musicodramatic scene.

In order to use songs and orchestral music in accordance with the content of the scene and the dramatic situation, songs which match the characters' personalities and music which matches the emotional colours of the events must be used. There is no song which accords with all times and all places. An opera requires music which suits the characters' personalities and the dramatic situation. Although there are many songs in an opera, it must be considered that there is only one song which suits a particular character's personality and a particular event and situation.

In order to provide close unity between the music and drama it is also essential to use songs and orchestral music in a variety of ways by means of various techniques to suit the dramatic moment and situation and the changes in the characters' feelings. The musical interpretation of scenes must

101

be varied and logical. In order to present the music in a scene in a varied way, you must decide the moments in scenes which are appropriate for a song, orchestral music or *pangchang*. Even the same song gives a different musical interpretation to a scene according to whether it is sung as a solo or chorus. The same is the case with orchestral music; it varies with instrumentation. It is only when these problems are solved in accordance with the dramatic moments and situations and the characters' psychological states that variety can be provided in the musical interpretation of scenes.

In order to ensure a close alliance between drama and music, the orchestra must link the scenes skilfully. The music in scenes alone cannot provide a full solution to the problem of an alliance between music and drama. A scene in an opera is the continuation of the previous scene and a precursor for the next scene. In the course of the steady heightening of the drama from one scene to the next, the characters' personalities develop and the theme of the work is further revealed. In opera the music must deal skilfully with the connection of scenes and the continued heightening and development of the drama.

(3) Emotional Delineation Is the Main Aspect of the Organization of Musical Drama

Emotional delineation is a method of representation which reveals the essence of a character's personality emotionally while showing his emotional world in a natural way in accordance with the logic of life. A man's feelings are based on life and change continually as life changes and develops. In the course of shaping one's life, one experiences various feelings, and their combination forms one's emotional world.

It is a basic requirement arising from the nature of art to explore man's world of feelings, his emotional world.

Opera provides a musical interpretation of a living man's concrete thoughts and feelings and the emotions arising from life. That is why music is called an art of emotions. In opera the characters' personalities and lives can be portrayed more impressively only when the method of showing their inmost selves is employed and their thoughts are brought out through strong emotions. In opera, unless the characters' inmost depths are revealed in full, they cannot be depicted as living men; and unless their thoughts are brought to light through their emotions, the portrayal cannot avoid being abstract. All the artistic requirements of opera can only be met in full through the skilful delineation of emotions. In operatic creation, therefore, emotional delineation must be regarded as essential in the organization of the musical drama, and all the songs and orchestral music must follow the line of the emotions.

Ensuring that the songs and orchestral music follow the line of the emotions means that various emotional changes in the course of the characters' actions are linked into one musical sequence in accordance with the logic of life.

To ensure that the songs and orchestral music follow the emotional line it is essential skilfully to weave the sequence of emotions that underlie the characters' lines of action. When there are ups and downs in life, emotions are bound to change; and when life develops continuously, emotions are bound to change continuously, going through the process of strain and relaxation, build-up and qualitative leap. This means that when there is a line of events in the drama, there is also the line of emotions which follows it. When the sequence of the characters' emotions of different colours arising from the events is linked into one musical sequence, the opera songs and orchestral music can be said to have been put on the emotional line. The characters' inmost depths must be penetrated in order to grasp the line of their emotions that arise from the events. You cannot grasp the emotional line if you are preoccupied with major events alone in the interests of dramatism, instead of exploring the characters' inmost depths. Even when dealing with a small or ordinary event, the composer must know how to penetrate and experience the inmost self of the character who is living through it.

When the composer has grasped the emotional line emanating from the line of the events, he must tune all the songs and orchestral music in keeping with the sequence of emotions. Opera songs and orchestral music must always be in tune with the most leading and essential emotion the character experiences when he encounters an event. Only then will the opera delineate the emotions in music, penetrating the character's inmost depths and clarifying the theme.

An important factor in keeping the music on the line of the emotions is to provide preconditions and moments in life that occasion the characters' actions, and to build up and develop their feelings by means of songs and orchestral music. In order to build up and develop the characters' emotions by means of music, their psychology and the emotional atmosphere must be shown deeply from various angles at the moment when the line of their destiny alters. That moment is a dramatic phase in which their accumulated emotions are brought to a head. In opera such moments must be penetrated by songs and orchestral music, and a proper musical timbre chosen to accord with the psychology of the characters and the emotional atmosphere. When I say that a proper timbre of music should be chosen to be in tune with the moment when the line of the characters' destinies alters, I do not imply that it must be changed at each moment without a unified plan for the whole course of the development of their personalities. It is natural that the characters experience vicissitudes in their lives, but they always experience them in particular situations. Therefore, at the moment when the line of a character's destiny alters, the music, while being used in a varied way, must become a part of the unified structure of the characterization. The variety of musical timbre which is used at the moments when the line of a character's destiny changes is inconceivable apart from the manner in which the elements of musical interpretation are used. Composers must explore the situation in the scenes and the inmost depths of the characters at such moments and choose appropriate means and methods of portrayal.

(4) The Musical Line Must Be Established

Since opera is a dramatic art that employs music as the principal means of portrayal, the musical line must be established. A distinct musical line in opera can make the structure clear, reveal the depths of the ideological content of the work emotionally and harmonize the interpretations of all the songs and orchestral music.

In order to establish the musical line in opera, it is necessary to provide a theme melody and make it run through the whole representation.

A distinct theme melody running through the operatic representation can make it possible to establish the musical line, unify the musical interpretations and keep the audience's interest and expectations alive at all times. For the establishment of the musical line and for making the theme melody permeate the whole of the operatic portrayal, the theme song and other excellent songs must be repeated at important moments of the dramatic development.

Repeating the theme song and other excellent songs at important moments is a fundamental method of organizing the musical drama so as to establish the musical line and make the theme melody penetrate the representation. This technique is important in intensifying the impression made by the songs, portraying the personalities of the major characters, describing the process of their development and unifying the modalities of music. In conventional operas using excellent songs repeatedly was inconceivable because stanzaic songs had not been introduced. The introduction of stanzaic songs in the new operas and the repetition of excellent songs when needed have blazed trail of musical dramaturgy and enhanced the popular character of the opera.

When repeating the theme song and major supporting songs the requirements of dramatic structure must be taken fully into account so that these songs are used in the scenes where the main thought of the opera is given intensive expression. *Song of the Sea of Blood,* the theme song of the revolutionary opera *The Sea of Blood,* is repeated three times: first, it is played as a prelude, giving a hint to the seed and leading the audience into the world of drama; second, it denounces the bestial atrocities of the Japanese imperialists by being played by the orchestra and sung as a *pangchang* in the scene of the massacre by the Japanese imperialists and in the scene in which Yun Sop is burnt alive; and third, it describes the fighting spirit of the people who resist the Japanese imperialists by being sung as a solo by Kap Sun and as a grand *pangchang* in the scene in which Ul Nam is killed. This method of representation, unlike the techniques of conventional operatic musical dramaturgy, fully accords with the logic of life and of representation. The death of Ul Nam is inconceivable separately from the death of his father, Yun Sop. It is the Japanese imperialists who brutally killed the father, and it is also the Japanese imperialists who killed Ul Nam. The sacrifice of their lives was for the sake of the country and the nation, for the sake of the revolution. The scene of Ul Nam's death, the epitome of the situation in Korea in those days when the whole land was a bloodbath, is a serious dramatic scene which sheds light on the truth of the revolution that where there is exploitation and oppression, there is resistance and the struggle of the people. If another song relating to the death of Ul Nam, not the *Song of the Sea of Blood,* is sung in those scenes, the tragedy of the family cannot be shown in one unified musical sequence, nor can it clarify the profound thought that Ul Nam's death is not the death of an individual but the misfortune and suffering of the whole nation. Because the song which was sung so bitterly in the scene of the massacre, in the scene where Yun Sop was burnt alive, is repeated by Kap Sun as a solo and as a grand *pangchang* in the scene of Ul Nam's death, the audience, thinking not only about the death of Ul Nam but also about Yun Sop's sacrifice, boils with resentment at the Japanese imperialists who have killed both the father and his son and plunged the whole village and the whole country into a sea of blood.

Furthermore, the audience is moved to think a great deal by the song *You Have Brought Medicine for Your Mother* in the revolutionary opera *The Sea of Blood,* which Kap Sun sings while embracing Ul Nam, who has bought medicine for his mother by selling the fish he caught, just before he is killed by the enemy. The melody of that song is that of the song *Don't Cry, My Dear Ul Nam* which his mother, with him, an innocent, suckling baby, on her back, used to sing quietly as a lullaby with Kap Sun, and a meaningful melody which is played by the orchestra for the future of young Ul Nam at the time when his mother, bereaved of her husband, was wandering from place to place. By repeating the heartrending song for the last time just before his death, Kap Sun makes his death seem more tragic. Thus, it is only when the theme song and the major supporting songs are repeated to tell of the eventful story of the principal character's life at important stages of the drama that they add to the philosophical depth of the interpretation and emphasize the ideological content of the work.

The theme song and the major songs that support it must be repeated at important moments which show the development of the characters' personalities. These songs have deeper meanings, cover a wider scope of portrayal and rouse richer emotions than any other songs; so when they are repeated at those moments, they can describe more vividly the process of the development of their personalities and the shaping of their revolutionary outlook on the world. If they are needed to show the characters' inmost thoughts and feelings and develop the drama they can be repeated even within a single scene in various forms. The melody of the song *It Is an Honour to Be Alive or Dead on the Road of Revolution* is repeated in different forms within the one scene of departure in the revolutionary opera *Tell O Forest* so as to describe the character's inmost depths and to add momentum to dramatic progress.

An operatic representation can be improved or impaired and the general sequence of the music can sound interesting or dull depending on how the songs are repeated. Therefore, songs must be repeated in a proper manner. Dealing properly with the repetition of songs is a creative process that requires thinking, inquiry and skill. If it is necessary to repeat songs, the logic of dramatic progress must first be considered carefully, and then the scenes where they should be repeated must be determined and the songs and the situation in the scenes must be allied closely with each other. If repeated songs do not suit the situations, they will sound superfluous; such a repetition will not be as good as providing new songs. Opera songs that are repeated must be seasoned with new flavour. Since the events and situations involved in the dramatic development do not repeat themselves, the songs that justify repetition must be developed and used in different forms and by different methods so as to produce a new flavour, as the logic of life requires. When the theme song is to be repeated, the theme melody can be re-arranged for the purpose or a song derived from that melody can be sung. When altering the melody, the original timbre must be preserved. The theme song and other excellent songs must be used in such a way as to retain and stress their original timbres despite being repeated in a varied fashion.

In addition to stage songs, the *pangchang* and orchestral music should be used widely for the purpose of repetition. The employment of the *pangchang* along with stage songs in various ways can increase the variety of the music, and the use of orchestral music produce a variety of emotional tones beyond the reach of vocal songs. No matter how a song is repeated, it must agree with the characters' personalities and the situation in the scene. This is the way to create a realistic musical interpretation.

In order to establish the line of opera music, it is essential to position songs and orchestral music properly and weave them closely.

It is an important principle in the organization of the musical drama of *Sea of Blood*-style operas to position songs and orchestral music properly and organize them carefully to accord with the characters' personalities, the logic of life, the content of the scene and the requirements of the situation. The observance of this principle can sustain the music itself, establish a correct musical line, form a consistent flow of emotions by means of songs and orchestral music and forcefully promote the drama. It can also show the depth of the development of the characters' personalities and create a clear musical interpretation of the theme of the opera.

In organizing the musical drama, creative workers occasionally deviate from this principle and emphasize their subjective points of view or the so-called logic of music itself. This shows that they are not yet completely free from the old concept of musical dramaturgy. In conventional operas it was a set pattern to include a few recitatives before the aria sung by the hero, and to include an arioso after the aria. A departure from this pattern was considered a violation of the rules of musicodramatic organization. Such a pattern can result in a separation of the content from the form in art. In opera the logic of music must always be based on the characters' personalities and the logic of life. There can be no logic of pure music separated from the characters' personalities and life.

Opera songs and orchestral music must always be positioned and woven closely together to accord with the characters' personalities and the logic of life. Like the storyline of other forms of dramatic production, the plot of an opera consists of presentation, development, climax and resolution, involving the processes of strain and relaxation, build-up and qualitative leap. In opera these processes of representation must be realized through the music. Therefore, music must strain or relax the dramatic situation and build up the emotions and lead them to a climax. In this it is important to place the stage songs, the *pangchang* and the orchestral music in their proper positions, overlapping and linking them so as to form a single musical sequence. Only then can the opera songs and orchestral music agree with the logic of the development of the drama, and promote the drama forcefully.

In order to establish the line of opera music you must use songs and orchestral music scrupulously. If you use them inappropriately, they will sound similar to one another, obscure the characters' personalities, weaken the musical impression made on the audience, cause the musical flow to become monotonous and relax the dramatic tension.

The use of many songs does not necessarily result in an excellent opera. You must not try to use a new song in every scene, simply because you have stanzaic opera songs at your disposal. Even in an opera of stanzaic composition, songs must be used sparingly. Experience shows that even in an opera of stanzaic composition, man and life can be described magnificently by means of only a few dozen songs. The musical line can be established in an opera only when the songs are not used at random but put in their proper positions, and the overall representation is run through with the theme melody.

An opera requires a good prelude, good music for the climax and a good finale.

The first impression of an opera depends on how the prelude is used, and the magnitude of the excitement an opera generates depends on the finale. An opera, no matter how good its content, cannot draw the audience into its drama unless the first impression made by the prelude is good; and the good impression it gives the audience will fall flat unless the finale is impressive.

The prelude must present or suggest the opera's theme and

the events in it on the basis of the theme melody and major supporting songs. The use of these songs in the prelude is very important in leading the audience into the world of the drama before the curtain rises. Only when the prelude characterizes the personality of the hero by presenting or suggesting the theme of and events in the opera can the audience receive an idea of the topic of the opera, identify the hero and become interested in his destiny while being drawn into the world of the drama. A prelude which is based on the stanzaic theme song and stanzaic supporting songs can draw the audience into the drama more quickly than the prelude of conventional opera because it has a succinct and plain musical structure and communicates its message clearly.

The prelude must be varied and idiomatic, according to the content and mood of the opera. Depending on the opera, the prelude can be performed by the orchestra alone or by a combination of the various forms of songs and orchestra. In such revolutionary operas as *The Sea of Blood, The Fate of a Self-defence Corps Man* and *The Song of Mt. Kumgang* the prelude is played by the orchestra alone. Even when the prelude is played only by the orchestra in our new operas, it is not only succinct and clear in its form but also familiar to the audience because it is derived mainly from the melody of the theme song of the stanzaic composition.

The prelude to an opera should also comprise songs of various forms and orchestral music in combination. Since the prelude to an opera is aimed at presenting the theme and giving a hint to the coming events before the curtain rises, methods of interpretation appropriate to the purpose must be adopted.

The preludes to *Sea of Blood*-style operas have taken on a new form which combines orchestral music with the *pang-chang* and several other forms of vocal music. In the revolutionary opera *The Flower Girl,* orchestral music in the prelude is combined with a song by the heroine and the *pangchang.* In the revolutionary opera *A True Daughter of the Party,* orchestral music in the prelude is combined with the *pangchang.* The prelude to *A True Daughter of the Party,* which comprises orchestral music and the *pangchang,* brings out the theme clearly from the outset and draws the audience into the world of the drama, while heralding a heroic act by the principal character. Whether the prelude should be performed only by the orchestra or with a combination of orchestral and vocal music should be decided according to the content and mood of the opera. If the prelude to a lyrical opera resounds with roaring and confusing sounds or if the prelude to an epic opera is performed only in gentle tones, it will conflict with the content and mood of the opera.

The music for the climax to the opera must be used properly. In the past the question of the standard for and principle of using music at the climax of the opera was interpreted in several ways. When *Sea of Blood*-style operas were being created for the first time in our country, some people insisted that the style of an aria or recitative should be used for the climax, claiming that this type of music was strongly dramatic, while some people were reluctant to use the theme song or supporting songs on the ground that a new song that conforms with the situation must always be used at the climax.

Now that stanzaic music has been introduced into the opera, the music for the climax must make effective use of the characteristics of the stanzaic songs. The melody of the song *Faith Moves Mountains* in the revolutionary opera *The Flower Girl* and the melody of the *Song of the Sea of Blood* in the revolutionary opera *The Sea of Blood* have a strong impact on the audience because the dramatism of these theme and supporting songs welds with the dramatism of the scene of the climax.

A new song can be used at the climax of an opera, but it is still better to repeat the theme song or a supporting song to suit the situation. In repeating these songs at the climax, the dramatic effect must be sustained by combining various means of musical interpretation according to the dramatic requirements of the climax. At the climax, intercommunication between the characters should be realized by using the theme song or a supporting song in accordance with the requirements of the situation and with the flow of the characters' emotions, and the freedom of characters should be ensured by means of the *pangchang* in the scenes where it is needed. A *pangchang* should be sung at the moment when a character's action is more important than his song. At the climax various forms of music can be used, but they should be fused by orchestral music. Only when the stage is brought to life in this way will the climax be sustained.

The finale of an opera must be used skilfully. It draws the theme of the opera to a conclusion and also concludes the events. It is the final music, and it depicts the characters' future destiny. Success in drawing an opera to a conclusion depends upon the finale.

The form of the finale and the methods of its interpretation may vary in different operas; however, it should always emphasize the theme of the work and have a strong lingering emotional effect on the audience. It should have greater depth, breadth and impact than any other music in any other scene. The finale of an opera must not be like the finale of a music-and-dance epic or the finale of a song-and-dance ensemble. Music-and-dance epics often end with a chorus which is combined with a magnificent dance. But the finale of an opera must not do so. The dramatic flow from climax to resolution in an opera is different from that in a music-and-dance epic and so is the resolution of the hero's destiny. The finale must, therefore, be suited to the content of the drama.

The finale of an opera should make effective use of the grand chorus and grand *pangchang*. The grand chorus plays a major role in sustaining the finale. In the finale the moment when the dramatic events are resolved, the process by which the characters' fates are settled and the emotional colours of the last part should be carefully analysed, the forms of the vocal should be determined accordingly and the orchestral music be properly ordered so that they produce a harmonious combination. Only then can all the musical means display their characteristics in completing the portrayal of the finale.

In opera the prelude and finale, the introductory scene and the last scene, must be linked artistically with each other. The prelude must present the theme of the work and the finale must bring it to a clear conclusion. The prelude to the revolutionary opera *The Flower Girl* and its finale set an example in dealing with them. In its prelude the introductory melody of the theme song *When Spring Comes Every Year*, which is played by the orchestra, gives a symbolic hint to the sorrow of our people who were deprived of their national sovereignty and their aspirations to a happy future; and then, the heroine's song and the grand *pangchang* say that beautiful flowers blossom every spring on the hills and in the fields, inviting the audience to hear the grievous story of why Ggot Bun has to sell these flowers. In the finale the melody of this song is repeated but the song sings with jubilation of the dignified and happy life of the heroine who has won freedom in the warm sunshine and is sowing the seeds of revolution. The song is sung only twice in the opera, as the prelude and finale, but it renders an active contribution to presenting and clarifying the profound seed that the flower basket of sorrow and filial duty becomes a flower basket of struggle and revolution. As you can see, the prelude, finale and the music at the climax should be used in a consistent manner in keeping with the logic of life and portrayal; only then can they sustain the musical line, depict the characters' personalities, develop the drama and bring out the theme to the full.

(5) The Mood of the Music Must Be Coordinated

Coordinating the mood of the music is very important in providing unity of operatic portrayal. A work with distinct mood can sustain the emotional tones of life vividly. The mood of opera music is defined in the libretto. Nevertheless, an opera becomes unidiomatic unless the timbre of each piece of music is sustained. If you are to produce an idiomatic opera you must make effective use of musical timbre. Coordinating the mood of opera music does not mean coordinating the timbre of all the musical pieces included in an opera. It would be impossible to weave a legitimate drama with serious and solemn music alone, or a comedy with light and satirical music alone, or a tragedy with doleful music alone. There are joy and sorrow, laughter and tears in human life. Works of art represent various aspects of life. That is why a work of opera with distinct style includes different musical timbres. Only when each song and each piece of orchestral music are idiomatic enough to match the real tone of life can the emotional colour of portrayal be sustained. However, even though different songs have different characteristics and produce different emotional colours, they will not prove idiomatic unless they are welded into the general mood of the work. The complicated creative work of coordinating into one mood the emotional tones of the songs and orchestral music which are performed at different stages of the dramatic development can only be successful when the musical drama is organized skilfully.

In order to sustain the mood of the opera music, it is essential to make the mood idiomatic by means of the theme song and to harmonize other songs and orchestral music with the theme song and theme melody. The idiomatic timbre of an individual interpretation can remain alive only within the harmony. The unity of mood can be ensured only when all the songs and orchestral music harmonize with the theme song and theme melody while retaining their peculiar timbres.

If the consistency and unity of the mood of the opera music is to be ensured, the theme melody should be sustained not only by being used at important dramatic moments but also by generating derivative melodies. Deriving other melodies from the theme melody is an important method of portrayal for realizing the contrast and unity of music in an opera of stanzaic songs. In an opera, the contrast and harmony of the overall musical interpretation and the unity of their mood can only be achieved when the various melodies are derived mainly from the theme melody. Composers must be skilful in this technique and still compose masterpieces. An opera can touch the heartstrings of the people only when its various songs and its orchestral music, with their peculiar emotional colours, are coordinated harmoniously into one mood.

4. OPERA DANCE

1) THERE SHOULD BE DANCES IN AN OPERA

Dance is an important means of operatic portrayal. The ideological and artistic qualities of an opera can be enhanced by meaningful and beautiful dances. Dance was not regarded as an indispensable component of operas of the past. The means of portrayal employed in works of art may vary with the characteristics of the genre and the intention of the interpretation. But in employing the means of portrayal full consideration must always be given to the particular aspect of life to be interpreted by art and literature and to the people's aesthetic tastes.

Life provides subject matter for art and literature; it also defines their forms and methods. Art and literature which depict life realistically should employ the forms and methods required by life.

The contemporary requirement of art is that, in step with the development of our life in its variety and richness, the role of the group form of art should be enhanced and that individual genres be combined to create a new group form of art.

Theatrical art in our country is creating a new form of art combining music and dance. This form is now used widely in song-and-dance ensembles and is developing into such an independent form of theatrical art as music-and-dance epics and music-and-dance tales. Creating a group form of theatrical art is a trend in the development of art in our times. This is an expression of a positive aspiration towards portraying the life of the popular masses, who are working enthusiastically for the revolution and construction, in greater depth and breadth.

Introducing dance into opera is a means of widening the scope of portrayal to meet the requirements of life and cater to the people's aesthetic tastes. Dances in an opera enable the opera to depict people's lives, thoughts and feelings in greater variety and richness and add a unique colour to the stage interpretation. Dance, with its own peculiar language, can delineate vividly what cannot easily be described by other genres. In the opera that has the task of representing life realistically on the stage, even the music and stage art can produce greater effect only when they are combined with dance. Just as life has various aspects, so the opera comprises different images and variety in its drama. Thus it is loved by the audience. If only songs are sung on the stage continuously, the drama will flow monotonously no matter how rich the songs are in their timbres. But a dance performed at an appropriate moment will create a change in the dramatic flow, adding to the variety of the stage representation.

Dances, showing the life portrayed in an opera profoundly in various aspects and changing the dramatic flow by various methods of interpretation, render the stage more colourful. When a dance is performed in an appropriate scene to suit the hero's personality and the requirements of life, the dramatic flow will be portrayed much more colourfully, by melodies and rhythmic movements alternately. It will also bring about a fresh change in the music and make the costumes, hand properties, sets and scenes more varied. Further, it will create harmonious formal beauty, revealing

119

beautiful and magnificent scenes on the stage.

Dances make an active contribution to portraying the characters' thoughts and feelings and their lives, bringing out a work's theme, and to making the stage colourful.

The revolutionary opera *The Song of Mt. Kumgang* reveals a vivid picture of the happy and fruitful life of girls working in the countryside because it has made the best use of dance. It realistically depicts, through dances, the happy and worthwhile life of girls picking medicinal herbs and apples while running an art circle, and provides a colourful description of the realities of a socialist rural village which has developed into a paradise. Various means of interpretation have been employed in the scene that shows the girls' labour and cultural life. But it is the dance that plays the main part in bringing out the content of the scene and in enriching the image. This testifies to the fact that dance is not a mere insertion that may or may not be included but an important component, and a powerful means of enhancing a work's ideological and artistic value and brightening the scenes.

Dance in an opera is congenial to the aesthetic tastes of our people who are fond of artistic forms that combine songs and dances. Our people make their work-places and lives merry with songs and dances. Likewise, they enjoy art that combines songs and dances. That is why the form of song-and-dance performances has developed and is now widespread. Operas can create truly popular stage images only when they use dances that conform with the centuries-old customs of the optimistic and beautiful life of our people and their ennobling aesthetic tastes.

The experience gained in creating *Sea of Blood*-style operas clearly shows the important role played by dances in furthering the artistic quality of opera and catering to the people's noble aesthetic tastes.

2) DANCES MUST MATCH THE DRAMA

In opera dances should match the drama if they are to play a depictive role. An opera needs dances which keep pace with the dramatic development, describing the thoughts and feelings of the characters and their lives. In conventional operas dance was, in most cases, merely an episode or an insertion for creating an atmosphere in scenes and stimulating the interest of the audience. As it did not belong to the dramatic plot, such dance could not play its proper role in furthering the ideological and artistic qualities of the opera.

It is only when the dances match the drama in an opera that they can become an essential component of the stage performance and play an active part in emphasizing the ideological content of the opera and improving its artistic quality.

Opera dances must be used only in important scenes.

That dances must match the drama in an opera means that dances must be used in scenes in which the drama develops. Dances must not be used at any time and in any scene in the opera; they must be used in those scenes that are important in the development of the drama. Music is the main means of operatic interpretation. But not every scene can be portrayed by music alone. In opera some aspects of life should be portrayed by songs and orchestral music, speeches and actions, and some by dances. Music or dance must be used as the scene requires. In art and literature employing means of portrayal to suit the life is the principal factor in realizing the unity of content and form and creating a realistic artistic portrayal. In opera, dance must be used in those scenes which cannot be depicted by other means of portrayal or which can

121

be interpreted better by dance than by other means. If scenes can be portrayed perfectly by other means, then you need not take the trouble to use dance. Dances which are performed in the right scenes can prove valuable.

Opera dances must be used in scenes as the drama requires, depict the characters' inmost thoughts and feelings and their lives in a diverse and profound way and thus influence the development of the drama.

It is a major function of opera dance to provide a rich description of the characters' inmost depths.

Dances must focus their attention on portraying the hero's inmost thoughts and feelings. As in all other forms of art, the ideological and artistic level of an opera depends upon the portrayal of the hero, and the value of the means of interpretation is defined by how it serves the depiction of the hero. Dances, too, can prove valuable only when they facilitate the portrayal of the hero's inmost self. From the point of view of the relationship between the drama and the hero, dances must be subordinated to emphasizing the hero's inmost thoughts and feelings. The drama of an opera is always the hero's drama. The drama is unfolded and developed with the struggle and along the line of action of the hero who is opposed to the old and creates and defends the new; so dances must be developed in the context of the development of the hero's destiny. Dances must be based on the hero's life and match the development of his destiny; only then can they be combined with the drama and subordinated to sustaining the line of the hero.

Dances, while keeping pace with the development of the characters' destiny, must depict in depth the process of the gradual development of their ideological awareness.

The revolutionary struggle gives birth to a man of a new type and creates a new life. In opera, songs and orchestral

122

music flow and scenes change in accordance with the logic of the development of the lives of the hero and other characters. Dances must clearly depict the distinctive features of the beautiful and noble mental and moral qualities and the new life of the men of a new type who develop in the course of the struggle.

In order to produce an exuberant portrayal of the characters' inmost depths, dances must portray the thoughts and feelings emanating from their experience of life and the change of their psychology in a delicate and varied manner and, by various means of portrayal, transform their desires for and aspirations to life into vivid images. Dances must represent the characters' thoughts and feelings vividly and in detail and express them naturally by means of rhythmic movements.

A dance which depicts the characters' inmost thoughts and feelings must portray in depth the events which have a strong effect on the development of their personalities. Besides their present life, therefore, meaningful aspects of their life of the past which influenced their growth should be described in retrospect, as should their future life, the reflection of their ideals, in dreams.

Dances in an opera, while portraying the characters' inmost thoughts and feelings, must vividly depict their development into men of a new type.

In the scene of a moonlit night in the revolutionary opera *The Flower Girl,* the dance shows the piteous plight and sadness of the heroine who, having been sold, is to leave her ailing mother and blind sister while rich women are enjoying themselves on a swing in the moonlight, and thus portrays the unjust class society which is a "heaven" for the wealthy and a "hell" for the poor; the dance in the scene of a dream shows the beautiful wish of the heroine to lead a happy life in a new society free from exploitation and oppression, a happy life with her brother and sister who have been forcibly separated by the Japanese imperialists and the landlord. The dance in the last scene blesses the hopeful future of the heroine who has embarked on the road of revolution and describes her ardent desire for the liberation of the country. These three pieces of dance in the opera clearly depict the image of the heroine who has been condemned to every manner of misfortune and suffering under the colonial rule of the Japanese imperialists and who, finally, embarks on the road of revolutionary struggle with an ennobling desire to create a new society free from exploitation and oppression.

Dances in opera must not only portray the characters' inmost depths but also describe life truthfully. Dances may vary in their content and form, but they must portray the life reflected in the opera properly. This can facilitate the depiction of distinctive features of the period and the characterization of what is typical. Dances can be typical when they delineate the characters' lives and the period vividly. Dances must not emphasize political aspects only, without describing life in detail, simply because they have to depict the period. They should depict the distinctive features of the period through a graphic and detailed portrayal of life. They must portray life; only then can they become meaningful, an inseparable component of the drama, and fill the opera with lifelike and original images. The dances in the scene of a dream that deal with the hero's aspirations must also transform his beautiful ideals into graphic life. This will make them an inseparable part of the drama and emphasize the general image of the opera.

Dances must stimulate the development of the storyline of the opera. Keeping pace with the dramatic development, they should open up a new phase for what is to come and create an appropriate precursor drawn from real life for the following scene.

The dance in the scene at Mt. Paekdu in the revolutionary opera *The Sea of Blood* brings to an end the first part filled with the pitiful life of the heroine and provides a precursor for her new life in a village at the foot of Mt. Paekdu. The group dance *Song of General Mobilization* in the last scene provides a precursor for the heroine's calling of the people to revolution to develop into the next event of the village youth rising up in the sacred anti-Japanese struggle, following the guerrillas. Dances which promote the development of the storyline should, on the basis of the development of life, be used at those moments that are important for the dramatic development and must fit in with the context of the scenes.

3) THE PATTERNS OF DANCE MOVEMENT MUST BE GOOD

The patterns of movement are important for dances which delineate the ideas and feelings of people and their lives. It is only when these patterns are idiomatic that they can form a rhythmic sequence and the flow reveal realistic scenes of people's lives.

The most important aspect of choreography is to create idiomatic movement patterns. Without rhythmic movement patterns, a dance is inconceivable; a wrong composition of movement patterns will result in a poor dance. Rhythmic movement patterns are the lifeblood of dance.

In the production of dances primary attention must be paid to the choice and polishing of rhythmic movement patterns that are capable of portraying life properly. In particular, it is very important to choose meaningful and idiomatic movement patterns in creating dances for opera so that the mental world of the characters can be portrayed in conformity with the dramatic scenes. If movement patterns which can vividly describe the characters' thoughts and feelings and their lives are not chosen, an excellent dance cannot be created however well structured it is visually. Needless to say, a dance is not performed only by movements; the music and set design are also important components. But, for all that, a dance will be no more than mere decoration if the choice and polishing of the movement patterns are neglected, in expectation of assistance from stage art. A dance must be comprehensible only through its rhythmic movements set to music, even without the help of the stage set or hand props.

Movement patterns should be picked up from life. The language of the art of dancing is based on the movements of people in real life. The sources of dance movements are also provided by the various movements of living people. From among these sources dance movements should be chosen to suit the content of the dance and the situation in the scene.

Attempts to invent the language of dance, divorced from the people's lives, would end in a variety of mistakes. For example, a few dance sketches have tried to describe something symbolically, separated from life, by means of abstract movement, instead of portraying it realistically. The method of symbolism can be used in some works since it performs the artistic function of portraying the distinctive features and meaning of an object. But, separated from the people's lives, symbolism can only be an expression of the creator's subjectivism. The same can be said of an abstract portrayal. Abstraction is necessary in life when choosing what is universal and essential by deleting what is individual and

126

incidental. In art and literature, however, the essence of life is not expressed in an abstract concept but in tangible images. Abstract portrayal is a misguided inclination to escape from life and make the reality obscure and general.

Movements chosen from the people's lives must be given a rhythmic and formative gloss to express the content of the dance. Only then can those movements, performing the function of language which expresses the people's thoughts and feelings and their lives, become beautiful, rhythmic and formative movements which rouse the emotions of the audience. Lifelike movements selected from reality should be natural and original as well as having an artistic gloss.

It is very important to preserve Korean dance movement patterns.

This is essential in expressing national sentiments properly through dancing. Only by preserving Korean dance movement patterns will dances represent our people's thoughts and feelings and their lives truthfully and cater to their aesthetic tastes. In an opera whose music is based on national melodies, the dances must also be produced in our way on the basis of Korean dance movement patterns.

Our people have an excellent dance heritage that has been developed over thousands of years. Korean dances, which reflect our people's national sentiments, have peculiar features in their postures and movements, in their sequences and in their rhythms.

Generally speaking, Oriental dances involve more movements of the upper part of the body than movements of the lower part. In Western dances it is the other way round. Korean dances, too, are performed with relatively more movements of the upper part of the body. But this does not mean that Korean dances are formed of such movements alone. Korean dances, with the movements of the arms as the main part, move the whole body harmoniously by combining them naturally with movements of the feet. Precisely in this is the true idiom of Korean dances.

The excellent characteristics of Korean dances can also be found in the fact that there are more temperate movements than passionate ones. There are no excessive jumping movements in our dances. The movements are moderate yet dynamic, elegant and beautiful. Their excellent characteristics are expressed well in their movement patterns, which have been harmoniously polished and refined. Heaving the shoulders up and down or spinning round lightly while moving the feet up and down or dancing with swaying arms—they are all distinctive features of Korean movement patterns.

The folk dance, which has developed on the strength of the people's talents and resourcefulness, is the reservoir of the movement patterns of Korean dance. The folk dance is the source to be relied on in developing national dance. Ours is a homogeneous nation with the same cultural tradition, but in each of our provinces a variety of folk dances peculiar to it has evolved. The folk dances which reflect our industrious people's working life and their beautiful customs have characteristic movements which have been refined over a long period. We must choose from our excellent dance heritage movement patterns with a rich feel of national characteristics, and polish them to meet the requirements of the period and to cater to the aesthetic tastes of our people.

In choreography there should be no tendency of ignoring the characteristics of Korean dance in an attempt to copy Western dances or of adulterating it with the Western. If the movements of Western dances are copied, the distinctive features of Korean dance cannot be preserved, nor can modernism be achieved. The imitation of Western dance movements will not bring about modernism. You will be perfectly able to create modern dances from the movements of Korean dance.

The question of modernism in dance can be solved smoothly only when the peculiar features of Korean dance movements are sustained to meet the requirements of the period and cater to the aesthetic tastes of our people. To this end, graceful and gentle movement patterns should be combined with powerful and dynamic ones. In essence, Korean dance movement patterns are gentle, and yet they are strong in their visual representation and vivid in their dramatic lines of action. They can express a vibrant spirit in a graceful and gentle flow and gentle emotion in a dynamic flow. If the best use is made of the excellent characteristics of Korean dance movement patterns, new movement patterns which are dynamic and, at the same time, gentle can easily be created. The dance *The Snow Falls* is a masterpiece which is modernistic and has rich national colour, because it portrays life realistically in the graceful and dynamic movement patterns of Korean dance to conform with our people's feelings.

Good music is a prerequisite for good dance movement patterns. It is the basis on which good dance movement can be composed. A dance is created on the basis of not only life but also music. Both life and music are the foundations and the starting-points in the creation of a dance. Life provides material for the creation of a dance while music provides it with emotion and rhythmic movements. A musical piece is not only a foundation for the production of a dance but also a foundation for its representation. A dance can be staged only when it is set to music.

The choreographer must select a proper musical piece and, on the basis of it, compose dance movement patterns. He must not produce them without selecting a musical piece nor subordinate the musical piece to the dance by lengthening or shortening it. The movement patterns must match the ideological content and emotional shade of the musical piece and the sequence of its melody. A rhythmic movement discovered in life should become a melody in a musical piece, and the melody should become the movement pattern in a dance. When a dance movement pattern becomes a visual "melody", it can match the musical flow.

Opera music and dance are easily allied with each other because they are based on the same life. Nevertheless, dance movement patterns do not always come to life automatically when the dance is put to a melody. Although music and dance are based on the same life, they have their own independent spheres of portrayal; so the choreographer should have a full knowledge of the musical piece and create movement patterns that suit it. A choreographer who has a good command of music can create suitable movement patterns and polish them as required by the musical flow. In this sense, he can be called a composer who portrays a musical piece in dance movement patterns. On the strength of a rich creative imagination, he must polish the material provided by life and the movements suggested by the music so as to create idiomatic movement patterns.

The opera stage must present excellent dances which have been refined to suit the musical piece, are full of national sentiments and are formed of beautiful and idiomatic movement patterns.

4) DANCES MUST BE IDIOMATIC

The operatic interpretation of dances requires variety. A large variety of dance arrangements can ensure a realistic and broad operatic interpretation of life, provide people with a correct understanding of life and rouse great emotional interest.

If opera dances are to be varied, every dance must have its own distinctive features. Idiomatic dances can contrast with one another and produce a great variety of images.

Opera dances must be idiomatic not just in a single aspect of portrayal but in all aspects of their content and form. If any of the elements comprising the content and form is the same or similar to another, the dances will be reduced to stereotypes.

The six pieces of dance in the revolutionary opera *The Sea of Blood* are all different. They differ in their content as well as in their movements, sequences, music and stage art. This shows that only idiomatic elements of interpretation can be organized into a dance to give it vivid content and varied colour.

In order to create an idiomatic dance it is necessary to explore the character's life that is unfolded with the development of the drama. Since each scene in an opera presents a different phase of the character's life, it is impossible for you to create an idiomatic dance unless you explore his life. The various events in life are merely an objective precursor to the creation of idiomatic dances. Whether an idiomatic dance is created or not depends on the point of view from which the choreographer explores life. He must study the character's life closely so as to form a clear understanding of its characteristics, grasp the thoughts and feelings emanating from them and, on the basis of this, arrange an idiomatic dance. A fresh and idiomatic dance language can be discovered in the course of conducting a close study of life. Every dance language is based on life. Dance movements are composed on the basis of the habitual movements of people in real life, and the formation and composition of a dance are defined according to the way in which they act. The various changes in the formation of a dance and its different forms of composition are all derived from the positions held by people in life and from their actions. The sequence and structure of a dance are also woven in keeping with the process of their lives. It is only when a character's life is understood that idiomatic movements and composition, the sequence and structure of a dance capable of an original portrayal of the character's thoughts and feelings, can be discovered and, on the basis of this, a new dance created.

In the art of dancing, for which the means of portrayal is limited, it is not easy to coin a new language in portraying every dance. Therefore, a variety of languages of portrayal created in the course of developing the art of dancing must be closely studied, adopted and polished. In particular, attention should be paid to preserving the movement patterns and forms peculiar to Korean dances.

When creating a new form of dance or polishing the forms that are already in use, it is important to preserve their characteristics. Since dance is a visual art, its form must first be idiomatic. According to the events unfolded in an opera, a song and dance, a dance in a dream or a symbolic dance can be used, but each form should have its own distinctive features. When the event to be depicted by dance is complicated and contains various aspects several forms, rather than only one, can be used in combination. When combining several forms of dance, the principal form should be defined properly and its characteristics must be sustained.

A song and dance is distinguished from other forms of dance in that it requires the dancers to dance while singing. On its own, however, this form cannot be completely idiomatic. For it to be idiomatic, the singing and dancing must be in

132

good harmony. Just as the words have to be set perfectly to the music to make a song, so the singing and dancing must be in harmony to create a single interpretation. In this form the melody of the song must be the movement pattern of the dance, and the rhythm of the song, that of the dance. If a song and dance is to be idiomatic, the dance must be realistic. Song and dance is, by nature, one of the most lifelike forms of art that has developed in close combination with the people's working life. It can be idiomatic only when it delineates life and takes a lifelike form as required by its nature. The song and dance *Winnowing* in the scene at the watermill in the revolutionary opera *The Sea of Blood* is idiomatic because the worthwhile life of the villagers, who are assisting the anti-Japanese guerrillas, is depicted by means of a song and dance in good harmony.

The characteristics of the dance in a dream must also be sustained. It reflects what takes place in a character's dream, so it should be more fascinating than ordinary scenes. Nevertheless, it must not be portrayed as if it were a fairy tale. A dream dance and a fairy-tale dance are different not only in their moods but also in their methods of portrayal. A dance in a dream must represent the events taking place in the character's dream, vividly depicting his or her ideals and wishes through these events. In such a dance the imaginary aspects should not be given too much prominence and the realistic aspects ignored, and vice versa. It must show imaginary images of the beautiful life the character desires.

In order to produce idiomatic dances, the choreographer must display a high creative spirit and break new ground.

If he merely adopts previous successes and experience intact and sticks to established norms, instead of displaying a high creative spirit, he might fall prey to imitation and mannerism.

Some of the dances created recently repeat almost all the movements and composition that have already been used in other dances, as well as the method of contrasting the beginning, the middle and the end. In some of these dances even the same costumes and hand properties have been used again. A choreographer who has fallen prey to imitation and mannerism cannot create an idiomatic dance, even though a variety of events and a detailed production task have been defined.

The choreographer must penetrate life and create original dance movements. Every single movement must be novel and never repetitive.

Opera dances should be in good harmony, as well as rich in variety. If harmony is overlooked for the sake of the idioms and variety of dance, the stage portrayal may become desultory. The beauty of art is in the harmony of various images. Only when the stage is adorned with a variety of dances which are in beautiful harmony can the opera create a stronger impression on the audience.

5. OPERA STAGE ART

1) THE SETS, INCLUDING THE BACKDROPS, MUST BE REALISTIC

The sets and backdrops constitute the main elements in stage art. They provide a vivid image of the characters' personalities and their lives and play a major role in describing the characteristics of the period and social system and in sustaining the formal beauty of the stage.

The sets and backdrops of the opera stage also play an important role in that they overcome the limitations of the music, which cannot describe the reality visually.

Opera is a musical art but the audience, when enjoying an opera, pays attention primarily to the sets and backdrops. When they see a realistic and vivid scene, people will listen to the music and be drawn deeply into the drama and feel as if they are living the reality rather than sitting in theatre seats.

It is because they are vividly impressed by the stage setting and backdrop that they do not repress their admiration when, with the playing of orchestral music, a backdrop with the title of the prologue is seen on the stage.

Impressive sets and backdrops remain in the people's memory for a long time. Thus they play an important role in giving the audience a deep impression of the work.

Sets and backdrops should be developed continually so as to depict the different aspects of the rich life of our people today in a realistic way.

Our new operas must portray people who are struggling to lead an independent and creative life. This struggle is very serious and comprises various aspects. For an opera to describe the struggle of our people today, its stage setting and backdrops should be innovative. Contemporary life cannot be represented in a realistic and vivid way by the sets and backdrops of the conventional operas which divided life into a few stereotyped acts and scenes and knitted the storyline. The stereotyped sets and backdrops of the conventional opera cannot portray the content of our new opera properly, nor can they portray in various shades dances which are set to stanzaic songs and the dramatic development.

The sets and backdrops of the conventional opera do not cater to the aesthetic tastes of our people, either. An opera audience wants to see realistic scenes. It is desirous of seeing on the stage as beautiful and kaleidoscopic a panorama of nature as it sees in reality and fresh settings that are like real ones. But in many of the operas of the past the sets and backdrops were formalistic and symbolical and, after an act, there was a rush to close the curtain and turn off the lighting so that the scene could be changed. This resulted in the audience regarding the stage itself and the scene as conditional, and in the frequent disruption and distraction of their attention.

In the operas of a new type the sets and backdrops have been innovated to suit the aesthetic tastes of the people. They are realistic and, at the same time, they change continually in accordance with the characters' actions and changes in the situation. In other words, they can depict in a truthful and vivid way aspects of real life and the process of its change and development. So, on our opera stage we can see the magnificent image of Mt. Paekdu and a wavy forest of trees, the fields of cooperative farms swaying with rich crops and a port where fishing boats are returning with flags of a full load flying, a rural village with cosy houses standing in rows and the panorama of the grand and magnificent city of Pyongyang. The new opera stage art of the three-dimensional stage working on a conveyer system is characterized by the fact that the surroundings of each event are natural and true-to-life, irrespective of the continual change of the sets and backdrops and that, although one season is replaced by another and several years pass in a condensed manner, they are all convincing and mysterious.

The new style of stage art can delineate any change of nature in a varied manner and on a wide scale and any character's personality and life in a realistic and vivid way. This is one of the underlying factors that strengthens the emotional influence of our new opera. Creative workers, on the basis of the successes and experience achieved in the course of creating new operas, should further develop stage sets and backdrops artistically and technically.

Sets and backdrops should reflect the character's thoughts and feelings and the development of his personality properly while creating realistic and lifelike surroundings for his life.

A man's personality and his life are inseparable. He builds and develops his life to conform to his aims and ideals. His personality is formed during the life he is building and is transformed and developed along with it. So a work of art or literature should portray a character's personality and his surroundings as being in an inseparable relationship.

In any work the surroundings must portray the appearance of the society at a given period and, at the same time, describe the personality of the character living and working in that society; only then will they become realistic and meaningful. Depicting life in a work is necessary to delineate the period and the personality of the character building his life.

The set and backdrop in the seaside scene in the revolutionary opera *The Flower Girl* in which Ggot Bun returns with her aim of seeing her brother, who is in prison, unfulfilled reflects in nature not only her unfortunate situation but also her resentment at her bitter experience. The angry sea and the waves beating upon the rock in this scene are the heroine's writhing and the explosion of the sorrow and anger brimming over in her heart. In this way the sets and backdrops of the opera stage must portray the surroundings of the character and his inmost depths.

In addition to depicting the characters' inmost thoughts and feelings, the sets and backdrops must delineate their influence on their surroundings. Only then can a more impressive appearance of the people who transform the world and shape their destiny be portrayed.

In the revolutionary opera *The Sea of Blood*, the stage set of the wall which splits as the mother, the heroine, opens the heavy gate of the walled town where the Japanese are entrenched portrays in bold relief the noble image of the heroine who has grown up into a new woman. It stresses that no wall and no obstacle can check the people's struggle.

The heroes in the operas of a new type are not passive people who adapt themselves meekly to the prevailing situation, but active people, like the heroine of *The Sea of Blood*, who transform the situation in accordance with their aspirations to and desires for an independent and creative life. Therefore, the sets and backdrops must portray truthfully the thoughts and feelings revealed in their transforming of life. This is the way to portray the personality of the characters in depth.

For the sets and backdrops to provide a delicate depiction of the characters' inmost thoughts and feelings, they must give visual support to the process of their growth while changing continually along with the current of life; they must also be transformed positively in conformity with the development of the drama. If they remain static, without changing in step with the dramatic development and the changes in life, they will not be lifelike. A change of backdrops, with the stage set fixed, cannot portray the surroundings realistically, either. Both the backdrop and stage set should be changed as much as possible so as to create lifelike surroundings. Objects which are in motion in reality should move on the stage. Changes in natural phenomena and in the surroundings should be presented on the stage in a natural manner. Even though such changes are artificial, they can become realistic if they are unaffected and agreeable to the aesthetic tastes of the people.

The sets and backdrops should be changed continually in such a way that they can portray in a varied manner changes in place and time. If the place of the characters' actions is fixed unnaturally or if a change in time is not depicted, the logic of life is ignored. Surroundings which do not change with a change in the characters' actions will be unrealistic and make no contribution to bringing out their personalities. Making wide use of the stage space, sets and backdrops should show successive events taking place in different places.

The time on the stage must change freely. If necessary, the change of time in one place—from sunrise to sunset or from dusk to dawn—should be shown in detail. If the change in time of the characters' actions is shown with the change in place of their actions, the flow of their life will become so much more natural.

Slide projectors have great descriptive potential for changing the scenes in a varied manner. They can present everything and all phenomena on the backcloth realistically. They can also vividly portray, without being limited by the

139

factors of time and space, complicated and diverse changes in life. The backdrops should be employed to create a variety of original and meaningful scenes by making full use of the descriptive potential of projectors. In making effective use of projectors, the background and setting should both be considered. If the projected scene and the scene setting are well combined, more diverse and vivid surroundings will be created on the stage.

Lighting plays an important role in changing the scene. The sets and backdrops will become artistic only when they are lit and coloured with the help of lighting. It can be said that the visual portrayal of stage art can be completed by lighting.

Lighting should be directed at the characters and all other objects on the stage as required by the plans for the depiction of the scenes. The question of where to focus the lighting, what to emphasize and what to change is not simply a technical matter but a matter of carrying through the plans for the portrayal of the scenes, so even a single light should be used with discretion.

Lighting should be focused on the character who is playing the principal part in order to underline the essence of the events taking place on the stage. In particular, it must show the hero most clearly along his action line. This will present the hero's personality in bold relief, emphasize the content of the events in the scene and draw the spectators' attention to the drama.

Through various changes, the lighting must provide a delicate visual depiction of the characters' mental state, the atmosphere of their lives and their emotions. It must show the characters' dramatic relations, make the surroundings vivid, create three-dimensional effects in the scenes and help to shift from one scene to the next by means of a contrast between light and shades and between different colours.

Stage art should also pay due attention to dealing with captions. Captions play an important role in sustaining the scene portrayal and in providing the audience with a clear understanding of the ideological content of the opera. The artist should have a correct understanding of the significance of captions in enhancing the descriptive quality of the opera and its popular character, and must make the best artistic use of the various forms of captions.

It is important to make the title caption of the opera impressive. The title of the opera plays no less important a role than the prelude in giving the audience its first impression of the opera. The prelude gives the first musical impression of the opera while the title caption gives it by graphic, visual means. The title of the opera gives a hint to its content and an idea of its mood. Thus it plays a role in guiding the audience into the world of the drama. Its style and colour and the way it is unfolded on the stage should accord with the content and mood of the opera. It should be succinct and strong in its visual expression.

The captions of the texts of the songs of the opera should be used properly. They play an important role in making the opera familiar to the audience and in strengthening the relations between the stage and the audience. The texts should be written clearly and harmoniously and in a neat and refined manner and displayed by stanzas as the songs are played.

Explanatory captions may or may not be used in an opera depending on the way the storyline develops. They should be used only if, without them, the context of an event is incomprehensible, the time and place are not clear or a specific explanation of the content is indispensable.

2) MAKE-UP PROMOTES CHARACTERIZATION

Make-up is an art which transforms the outward appearance of an actor so as to create a distinct visual portrayal of the character he is playing.

Make-up is an indispensable means of portrayal for an actor in the performance of his role. It gives him the appearance of the character he is to play. It enables him to identify himself with the character and to identify the character with himself. Only then can he enter into the character's feelings naturally and further his characterization not only through his words and actions but also through his appearance. A character's facial expressions on the stage can, as in life, expose his inmost self sensitively and delicately and, at times, reveal in vivid detail an intricate emotional state which cannot be expressed fully by words or actions.

Through the depiction of the outward appearance of the character, make-up reveals not only his inmost self but also his national characteristics, his class position, his economic status, the standard of his cultural life, his occupation and his age, and provides a general insight into his personality. That is why the audience distinguishes the personality of a character as soon as they see his outward appearance on the screen or on the stage.

If a character's appearance is to be convincing, his make-up should be true to life.

True-to-life make-up means make-up that suits the character's personality and life and the actor's physical features. In short, make-up must conform with both the character and the actor to be realistic.

If make-up is to be realistic, it should suit the character.

What is important here is to make up the outward appearance of the character on the basis of his inmost self and unify their portrayal. Certainly, a man's appearance does not always reflect his inmost self precisely, but his appearance bears traces of his past that cannot be erased. Also, every man dresses in harmony with his personality. Hence the saying: seeing the outside is seeing the inside. This means that the outward appearance of a character should reflect his inmost self. Depicting the outward appearance of a character on the basis of his inmost self and unifying their images is a basic guarantee for realistic make-up.

A make-up artist should begin his creative work by gaining a deep understanding of a character's inmost self and then, on the basis of this, proceed to the depiction of his outward image. In order to understand a character's inmost depths, he should pinpoint the main features of the character and the decisive factors in the depiction of his outward appearance. Make-up should emphasize the main features and depict changes in a character's appearance in a proper way, changes which take place with the development of his ideological consciousness. This is particularly important in making up a character who grows up in the course of the drama. It is difficult for an actor realistically to portray a character from his youth through to old age; it is no less difficult for a make-up artist to depict truthfully, through an actor, a character's appearance changing with the passage of time. When making up a character who ages in the course of the drama, a make-up artist should make him up to look young and old, but should consistently maintain his appearance of his young days, even though he goes through changes with the passage of time, until his elderly years. The characteristics of his personality revealed at each stage of his growth and the traces of his life should be well harmonized with his original characteristics.

It is natural that a man's life leaves traces on his appearance. Time and life have a great influence on the formation of a man's personality; their influence on his appearance is great as well. His features acquire different characteristics as time and life develop. Take a worker or a peasant for example. The worker or peasant of today differs from the one of yesterday not only in his spiritual and moral traits but also in his outward appearance. Make-up should select, from among various traces left by time and life on the appearance of the character, the essential features which can act on typifying his personality and depict them effectively. It is an essential characteristic of realistic make-up to portray the outward appearance of a character in relation to the period and his life so as to make his personality typical.

If it is to be realistic, make-up must suit the actor's physical features. Since make-up is the art of portraying a character on the basis of the actor's outward appearance, it can only be realistic when it accords with the actor's physical features. If it does not, his face might be deformed and his actions awkward. A make-up artist should make an actor up so that his outward appearance clearly describes his character's inmost depths and outward features. The artist should create a portrayal which matches the character and accords with the actor's physical features by emphasizing the elements of the actor which are similar to those of the character and by transforming and suppressing other elements.

To create realistic make-up, the conditions of the stage should be taken fully into account. Because of the role played by the camera and the characteristics of film, the cinema can present a close-up of a far-away object, magnify a small object

144

and show an invisibly minute object in a vivid image. So a cinema actor may be made up lightly. But in the opera, as the stage is distant from the audience, as that distance cannot be controlled freely as in the cinema and as the audience's focal point is always fixed, the actor should be made up so that his facial lines and profile are distinct and a clear visual image of the character is created.

In making up stage actors artistic exaggeration is necessary. Therefore, larger forms should be taken and lines and colours should be bold. Exaggeration in making up should not go to an extreme, however. Although make-up should be thick, faces should not glisten too much or the eyes be too large, and although noses should be sharp, the lines should not be too bold or the light and shade contrast too much. Excessive exaggeration breaks the harmony of a character's appearance and deforms his image.

Make-up should be beautiful. All the activities of a man who is transforming nature and society are closely related to his aspirations to beauty. He always tries to create a beautiful life and to look beautiful. Trying to create and enjoy beauty is a man's desire. Since an opera mirrors this aspiration, the hero and other characters should be made up in a beautiful fashion.

Creating beautiful make-up means making up a character in such a way that his outward appearance reveals clearly his inmost self and is full of vigour, and that his face and figure are in harmony.

Giving emphatic expression to a character's mental world is a fundamental aspect of make-up.

The face and figure alone should not be made up beautifully, at the expense of the beautiful mental world of the character. If a character's face is made up in this way in total disregard of the characteristics of his personality and the

145

conditions of his life, his outward appearance may not express his inmost self. Making up a character's face beautifully while neglecting his personality is an expression of formalism.

Make-up should always pursue the beauty which matches the character's personality. A worker should be depicted as giving off the smell of grease and a peasant the smell of earth and, at the same time, the beauty of a toiling man should be expressed in the depiction. Making up a character's face beautifully and his figure harmoniously should be subordinated to sustaining the beauty of his personality. Make-up should maintain the balance and harmony of a character's face and figure to conform with a character's mental world; only then can a man with a beautiful heart and appearance be portrayed.

Opera dancers should be made up well. The make-up of a dancer should accord with the characteristics of the art of dancing and be based on the principles observed in making up other stage actors. A character is made up according to his personality and outward appearance, but a dancer cannot be made up in this way. The dancers who dance as characters can be made up in this manner, but when they all portray the thoughts and feelings of one character, they should not be made up in this way. In such a dance their outward appearances should be unified into one typical image. In a dance depicting the thoughts and feelings of one character, harmony of representation can be achieved only when the appearances of the dancers are unified, because their costumes and hand properties are uniform.

3) COSTUMES AND HAND PROPS ARE A MEANS OF CHARACTERIZATION

Costumes and hand props play an important role in characterization. Even the costumes and hand props which are used once or twice have an effect on characterizing personalities, the times and the social systems, as well as on the development of the drama.

They should be used to suit a character's personality and his life.

A person's clothes and personal effects reflect his practical and aesthetic requirements. They are essential for him in his life; so when making them, he takes their practical and aesthetic value into full account. This means that in a work of art the costumes and hand props should be decided on and portrayed on the basis of the requirements of a character's life and his aesthetic needs. Therefore, they should not be dealt with perfunctorily, but on the basis of these requirements. If a worker is dressed in work clothes and given a hammer, and if a soldier is dressed in a military uniform and equipped with a rifle, the costumes and hand props will give, at the most, a general notion of the characters' occupations. Even work clothes and military uniforms reflect the individual tastes and preferences of the wearers, so costumes should not be handled perfunctorily.

Costumes and hand props should be used for the significant events which have a major influence on a character's life. In particular hand props should be used repeatedly at moments which are important in the development of the drama so that they emphasize a character's personality and develop the drama in depth. As a medium which links the characters in the context of their destiny and resolves these relations in an impressive way, and as a precursor to a new event, hand props should deepen the relations between characters and develop the storyline in an interesting way.

Costumes and hand props are of great significance in depicting the characters' social and class relations. In an opera which reflects life in a class society, the characters' social and class relations can be depicted clearly by means of costumes and hand props.

The class relations of people in an exploitative society are expressed, as in other aspects of life, in the clothes they wear and the personal possessions they use. Of course, clothes and personal belongings are mere articles, but they reflect differences in wealth. Therefore, an opera should depict the characters' class relations by artistically contrasting costumes and hand props. However, by this contrast alone it is difficult to depict the depth of a character's personality. Particularly in an opera which depicts life in a socialist society in which there are no class contradictions and people lead an equally happy life, the characters' social relations cannot be revealed accurately by the quality of their costumes and hand props alone. These social relations should be depicted by elements indicative of the personalities, as well as by their quality.

They should vividly reflect the distinctive features of the period and social system. Only then can they contribute to the portrayal of the representative personality of a character and give people a correct understanding of the period and social system. A man's attire and personal effects correspond to the level of development of the period and the characteristics of the social system, so they naturally reflect the features of the period and social system. In a capitalist society there is a style of dress and there are personal possessions which correspond to the characteristics of that society and the bourgeois way of life, whereas in a socialist society there is a style of dress and there are personal effects which correspond to the characteristics of that society and the socialist way of life. The style of dress in capitalist society follows fashion. So in this society people in general are foppish and wear showy clothes. On the other hand, in socialist society the masters of which are the popular masses, their clothing is characterized by beauty, nobility, soundness and serviceability. This is an expression of the feelings of socialist people who are revolutionary and industrious. So in opera the distinctive elements which can depict the appearance of the period and social system should be identified and applied to the use of costumes and hand props.

In opera close attention should also be paid to the employment of dance costumes and hand props.

Dance costumes and hand props should be used to suit the characteristics and content of the work. The costumes and hand props used in other dances should not be used repeatedly in disregard of the characteristics and content of the work, nor should inappropriate costumes and hand props be used on the ground of making them idiomatic. It is an expression of formalism to try to use luxurious costumes and expensive hand props which have nothing to do with the characteristics and content of the work; this should be strictly guarded against. As an opera singer should use costumes and hand props to suit his character's personality and life, so a dancer should use costumes and hand props to conform with the characteristics and content of the work so as to create a realistic portrayal.

The costumes and hand props of dancers should be idiomatic, according to the genre and form of the work. When a dancer dances while playing the role of a character, his costume and hand prop should match the personality of his

149

character and, accordingly, be distinguished from those of other dancers. But in a dance where several dancers portray the thoughts and feelings of one character, or in a dance which portrays the ideological content of a scene symbolically, the costumes and hand props should be unified.

The dancers' costumes and hand props, while fully satisfying the characteristics of the work, should accord with its content. Even the costumes and hand props of dances of the same genre should accord with their content. In every dance the costumes and hand props should conform with its content so as to portray it properly and improve its artistic quality.

In addition, the costumes and hand props of dancers should be convenient for dancing, capable of sustaining the rhythms, rich in their expressive power and beautiful. This is the difference between the costumes and hand props of dancers and those of actors.

Stage art should create impressive costumes and hand props which suit the personality of a character and the characteristics of the dance and, at the same time, make them harmonize with one another and conform with the sets and backdrops so that scenes of beautiful form can be unfolded on the stage.

4) THE PRINCIPLE OF REALISM MUST BE OBSERVED IN STAGE ART

In order to meet all artistic requirements in the creation of stage art, the principle of realism must be strictly observed. Only by doing this is it possible to eliminate the tendency of oversimplifying or formalizing sets and backdrops, exaggerating make-up or using costumes and hand props as mere ornaments, and to portray the characters' personalities and lives realistically.

In opera, unlike in the cinema, sets and backdrops can be simplified to some extent, depending on the objects, or formalized to a certain degree for the sake of the style of stage representation, or used for the sake of the decorative effect of the costumes and hand props, in consideration of the characteristics of the stage. However, if you exaggerate or beautify the images in stage art separated from the characters' personalities and lives, you may fall prey to formalism; if you present existing objects and people on the stage as they are, you may fall into naturalism.

Formalism in art and literature not only degrades the ideological quality of a work but also damages its artistic quality and nullifies its cognitive and educational functions; it does so by separating the content from the form and subordinating the former to the latter. Abstract artists do not know what they have drawn in their drawings. When people ask them what they have drawn, some of them answer that they do not know now that they have finished the drawing, even though they knew before drawing it, so I have been told. They claim that the less people understand the meaning of a picture when they see it, the greater a masterpiece it is.

Naturalism is anti-realism in the guise of realism. It is a trend of bourgeois art and literature which copies the reality mechanically and superficially and falsifies its essence on the pretext of reflecting the reality as it is. Naturalism, the reflection of the interests of the bourgeoisie, rejects the social and political evaluation and ideological and aesthetic evaluation of the reality, depicts the inessential, miscellaneous trivial aspects of life, being divorced from the principle of creating typical life, and portrays a man, a social being, like an animal. It is also an expression of naturalism to describe, in

151

the guise of figurative portrayal, only pure nature separated from social life. In the long run, it distorts the reality of life, abuses man's dignity and nullifies the social value of art and literature. These are the harmfulness and danger of naturalism.

Formalism and naturalism, which benumb the class consciousness of the popular masses, conceal the reactionary nature of the capitalist system and represent the interests of the exploiting class, have nothing in common with our revolutionary art and literature. We must on no account tolerate the slightest manifestation of formalism and naturalism, which reflect life falsely, hinder the advance of the revolution and check the sound development of art and literature. We must categorically reject them.

Stage art must present the make-up of characters, their costumes and hand props, houses and trees on the stage, and even a drifting cloud on the backdrop as realistically as we see them in reality, and also accurately reflect in them the personalities of the characters, the essence of life and the characteristics of the times and social system.

In the scene in the revolutionary opera *The Flower Girl* in which the sick heroine is grief-stricken after her vain journey to see her brother and, having been told that her brother is dead, goes with difficulty on her way back home after giving up the idea of suicide at the thought of her blind sister awaiting her, her tragic misfortune and her complicated psychological state are depicted in depth and the true nature of the cruel and callous life of that time is clearly revealed by such realistic and vivid details as the small house with the "INN" sign, the lonely telegraph-pole, the distant tunnel on the backdrop, the whistling train coming out of it and the dim light emitted from the train windows. This proves that the stage art of our new opera is a true art of realism which is as natural as reality, expresses the personalities of the characters and the essence of life and depicts the characteristics of the times and social system.

In order to depict the characters' personalities and life truthfully and create an interpretation which accords with the tastes of our people, stage art must preserve and develop the characteristics of excellent Korean painting so as to cater to the aesthetic tastes of our people today. Stage art should delineate their mental traits and the process of the deep-going changes taking place in the building of a new society, and accurately reflect our people's national characteristics which are newly enriched in the contemporary era. This challenge can be met only when new images suited to modern aesthetic tastes are created on the basis of the vivid and succinct traditional art of Korean painting.

In order to create new images in stage art, the successes of advanced science and technology should be introduced in every way possible. Images of stage art in our new opera cannot be created with the outmoded stage settings and technology of the past. The latest developments in science and technology should be introduced widely and put to rational use in all fields of stage art, which is a combination of sets, backdrops, lighting and other material and technical means.

In the introduction of these developments you must guard against technical routinism and the neglection of the artistic aspects of portrayal. The technology of the interpretation of stage art should serve the furthering of the ideological and artistic qualities of the opera.

The continued discovery of possibilities for fresh representation should be conducted in all sectors of stage art, and they should be used more effectively. If existing forms of stage art are presented unchanged or if conventional means and methods of representation are repeated, a new life cannot be shown in a fresh way, nor can stage art itself be innovative. Bearing deep in mind their responsibility in developing the art of the opera, artists should boldly rid themselves of the outdated way of thinking and methods of interpretation and continue to work out original methods of stage art.

6. OPERA STAGE REPRESENTATION

1) THE ACTING MUST SUSTAIN THE SONGS

The studies and efforts of the creative workers and artists who take part in the creation of an opera will bear fruit finally in the stage representation.

The creative work of the singers occupies an important position in completing the stage representation of an opera. An opera singer directly portrays a character's personality, the essential part of the stage representation. A song composed by a composer will become an audible musical piece only through the singer's characterization.

In the first place, an opera singer must sing well. A stage actor's main task is to speak and act well while an opera singer's main task is to sing well. Words and actions are a means of interpretation for an opera singer, but they cannot be compared to the role of song. The image of a character in an opera can come to life only when the singer sings well.

For the singer to sing well, he must understand and experience the depths of the personality and life of the character.

If he sings without a proper understanding and deep experience of his character's thoughts and feelings and life, his singing will not suit the character's personality. He must not think that he is singing well if he merely observes the technical rules of a musical score without gaining any experience of his character's personality and life. Without such experience he will find it impossible to create a truthful musical interpretation, even though he is faithful to the notation. Even singers playing the minor characters, to say nothing of those who play the parts of the hero and other major characters, must study the lives of their characters and gain experience of their thoughts and feelings. Although a character is to sing only one song, the singer must explore the course of his life, accept his thoughts and feelings as his own and live at all times in his world so as to interpret the song truthfully. Only a singer who lives in the character's world and experiences his life can regard himself as the character and fully explore his state of mind. The deeper a singer enters his character's personality, the more naturally he can sing with the feelings of the character and the more truthfully he can portray him.

Making a song's emotional key vivid is one of the basic ways of portraying it realistically to suit a character's personality and life.

The emotional key of an opera song is based on the mental state and life of the character singing it and reflects his feelings. Sustaining the timbre required by a song is an important guarantee for an emotionally idiomatic characterization. The more delicate the timbre is, the better a character's inmost depths will be brought out and the more lifelike his individuality and life will be represented.

In order to sustain the emotional key of a song, the singer must control his emotions well when singing.

When singing, some singer becomes full of emotion even before the emotional events unfold simply because he has to experience the feelings of characters; but the audience cannot follow his emotions. If he sings in this manner he can neither sustain the timbre required by the song nor truthfully interpret the character's inmost thoughts and feelings; he may even spoil the general delineation of the emotions. An opera song is sung in a particular situation in the development of the drama when appropriate events have taken place and culminated in an emotional climax. Therefore when singing, the singer must take fully into account the life experience of the character and the emotions which have been built up with the dramatic progress.

In opera the *pangchang* should be sung in accordance with its characteristics. It has some features which distinguish itself from stage songs. It differs from stage songs in its timbre and form. The singers of the *pangchang* can retain its peculiar colour and sustain the variety of musical interpretation by providing a clear contrast to the stage songs only when they sing it as its characteristics require.

For an excellent portrayal of the *pangchang,* it should be sung in clear and beautiful voices and in voices of great amplitude and resonance. Only then will it be full of emotions and distinct in its timbre. Making a sound is one thing and sustaining emotions is another, but they are in an inseparable relationship. When the voice is full and resonant the *pangchang* can express rich emotions. A voice that lacks amplitude and resonance cannot express rich emotions. The amplitude and resonance of the *pangchang* is proportional to the number of singers, but depends largely on the organization of the vocal parts and their singing.

It is important in the singing of the *pangchang* to meet the requirements of the function and form of the *pangchang*.

When the singers of the *pangchang* choir sing for a character, they take his stand; so, like the stage singers, they must have a proper understanding of the character and experience his inmost depths and, on the basis of this, sing with his feelings. They should live in the character's world as much as the stage singers do. A stage singer performs the role of one character and that is his entire role. But the *pangchang* singers have to interpret the thinking of several characters, so they should experience the thoughts and feelings of the different characters. Only a *pangchang* which flows out from a deep experience of a character's inmost depths can stress the character and touch the heartstrings of the audience.

The *pangchang,* or off-stage song, which, unlike the songs of the singers on the stage, represents the librettist's attitude towards the events taking place on the stage, and the narrative *pangchang,* which explains the social surroundings, natural scenery and the passage of time, should be sung in accordance with their characteristics so as to sustain the timbre required by the song and underline the stage portrayal.

The *pangchang* should be sung to suit the characteristics of its various forms. It can be sung by one or two singers or by a small, medium or grand choir to make it distinguishable from the stage songs. The point at issue is how to portray all the different songs idiomatically. When this problem is resolved the *pangchang* will be colourful and varied, emphasize the operatic images in keeping with the scene changes, and broaden the scope of the audience's emotional experience.

Singers should pronounce the words clearly so that their meaning is understandable. This can be done only when our own style of vocalism is applied. This means singing in a tender and natural, clear and beautiful voice as the emotions of the Korean people and their physiological features require.

In this regard, we must have a correct understanding of our folk vocal sound and the vocal sound of the West. Nobody now regards the husky voice of the *pansori* as a vocal sound that suits our national melodies. But some people still have the misunderstanding that only our folk vocal sound is our national style of vocalism. There are differences between our folk and Western vocal sounds, but there is no need to give prominence to either of them. Our folk vocal sound cannot produce the great amplitude of modern songs satisfactorily, and Western vocal sound cannot properly interpret a song which conforms with our people's feelings.

Singers must learn our style of singing in a tender and natural, clear and beautiful voice. When they sing in this way, national feelings will come naturally into life and the words of a song will be communicated clearly.

The harmony of opera songs should be realized. The small ensemble, chorus and grand ensemble in which different singers sing together have their appeal in the harmony of the amplitude and resonance of the musical performance. The vocal sounds of all the members of the *pangchang* choir should be harmonized to create a beautiful interpretation.

To this end the singers, on the basis of their experience of the characters' thoughts and feelings, should coordinate their vocalism, maintain an even tone and regulate the timbre. Artistic harmony can be complete not only when one aspect of the performance is harmonized but when the whole form and content of it is harmonized.

An opera singer must act skilfully while singing well.

He will neither portray a character truthfully nor sustain his song properly if his acting is confined to making some facial expressions or hand gestures, just as an ordinary vocalist does. The singer who becomes stiff on the stage and cannot move freely cannot easily become an opera singer even if his voice is beautiful and he sings well. Opera is a singing art, an acting art and an art of portraying life. Opera songs express the characters' thoughts and feelings in music and flow out from their lives. Just as an actor's speech is the act of expressing a character's thoughts and feelings, so is an opera singer's singing. Just as a character's actions are based on life and develop along with it, so his songs flow out from life and develop along with it. His singing in the opera is, in the long run, his acting and his living. In opera, in which songs and actions are closely allied on the basis of life, a living character can be portrayed vividly and life shown in a natural way only when the singer acts skilfully while singing.

A singer should act on the stage as naturally as he does in real life. He should not act in such a way that he acts only before he sings, but becomes too stiff to act when he has begun singing and resumes his acting only when he has finished singing, nor in such a way that he stands still before singing, starts acting when singing and finishes acting with the finish of his singing. A character's life in an opera proceeds consistently from the time of his appearance on the stage until the time of his exit, so he should show, with lifelike acting, the life before and at the time of his singing, and the life that lingers on after it.

The opera singer has to sing while acting and act while singing. This is similar to the method of depiction used by stage and film actors who speak while acting and act while speaking.

In particular an opera singer must act realistically while singing. In an opera, songs should have the support of actions to make the portrayal of a character vivid and strengthen the impressions and emotions emanating from the songs. The acting performed while a song is sung should serve to sustain the song. Both songs and actions express a character's thoughts and feelings. But acting is meaningful only when it contributes to emphasizing the thoughts and feelings emanating from the song. The singer should pay primary attention to singing and should act realistically to conform properly with the colour of the song and further its thoughts and feelings.

If the singing is to be supported properly by the acting, the distinctive features of opera acting should be understood. It is easy to act while speaking, but it is not easy to act while singing. So the opera singer, unlike the stage actor, should avoid complicated and minor movements, and follow a solid line of action consisting of meaningful movements which accord with the key of the song. A skilful actor portrays a character's personality properly even if he acts only a little, but an unskilled actor cannot express a character's personality properly even if he acts a great deal. An opera singer must have the skill of acting to enhance the song's interpretation and sustain a character's personality by making a few simple movements.

The movements made while singing should not be irrelevant to the song, nor should the acting be neglected by paying attention only to the singing. Only a singer who harmonizes his singing and acting can create a truthful characterization.

An opera singer must act realistically not only when he sings but also during the strains of songs and orchestral music. In an opera there are times when a singer has only to act, without singing. In some scenes a singer has to describe an event by his reaction to songs which are being sung by other characters and has to act to portray an event which is unfolding during the performance of the *pangchang*. In some scenes he can depict a character's thoughts and feelings more effectively by his acting than by his singing.

When a singer acts during the strains of songs and orchestral music, he should act in keeping with the musical rhythms as much as possible.

In opera, the drama exists in songs, and songs in the drama; likewise the acting should be performed to the music, and the music should penetrate the acting. It is only when a singer acts to the music and its rhythms that the acting becomes artistic and the music and acting harmonious.

Acting thus is the major characteristic of an operatic performance.

Although an opera singer has to act artistically to the music, he must not produce a rhythmic performance as dancers do, still less should he exaggerate his movements as the "new-school" actors of the past did. Exaggerated acting is revealed mostly in the performance of actors who portray villainous characters. Some singers who portray such villainous characters as a landlord or policeman are inclined to perform exaggerated, superficial actions, instead of singing well. Exaggerated acting is a remnant of the outdated "new school". What is worst in this school is to speak and act in an affected manner and produce an exaggerated appearance. A realistic character cannot be portrayed through a performance of this school, which depends on the use of affected words and exaggerated actions.

If an opera singer clings to exaggerated, formalized superficial acting, his singing, to say nothing of his portrayal of a character, will lose truthfulness. He should act in a natural manner in keeping with the thoughts and feelings flowing out from a song, and make every single one of his facial expressions and every single one of his movements realistic and vivid.

Dancers should dance properly. Everyone can dance, but it is not easy to dance artistically. Some dancers try to practise movements of a dance as soon as the choreographer finishes his design. As a result they fail to dance properly. Before practising individual dance movement, they must concentrate on a study of the choreographic production. Only then can they set the right direction for their performance, penetrate the depths of the work and become familiar with the correct movements.

The study of a dance should be conducted along the

162

character's line of life that corresponds to the development of the drama. There are various pieces of dance in an opera, according to the scenes, but they reflect the characters' thoughts and emotions and the events relating to their lives in the dramatic context. Dancers must know what requirement each dance reflects at which phase of the dramatic development, what relations it has with a character's life and what its ideological content and artistic characteristics are.

Dancers must penetrate the depth of the work by understanding its content, and become familiar with its dance movements by repeated practice, and then proceed to an intensive performance.

They should dance in a realistic and beautiful manner so that their performances overflow with national emotions. Creating a realistic dance is the main task of the dancer as well as of the choreographer. The beauty and national emotions of a dance are guaranteed by its faithfulness to reality. An unaffected, truthful portrayal is beautiful; describing the thoughts and feelings of our people and their life as they are is the way to underline national emotions.

A realistic and beautiful dance consists in harmony. A dance can be truthful and beautiful not only when its movements are natural and refined but also when it is harmonious.

The true harmony of a dance is realized through the unity of the aspirations and feelings of the dancers. The harmony realized through the mechanical unity of postures and movements is not, in its true sense, artistic harmony. The harmony of a work of art, though the work is well-structured, will not be truthful and beautiful if it is separated from the content. True harmony is achieved when all the dancers perform, breathing as one.

Dances can breathe in harmony only when they experience the thoughts and emotions of a dance and, on the basis of this, master the movements and the tune of the music. Dancing to the music is a precondition for realizing the harmony of a dance. A harmonious performance of dances can be achieved only when the ever-changing movements agree naturally with the postures and facial expressions.

In their performance dancers must sustain the characteristics of Korean dance in their movements and postures. Even though a choreographer has produced a dance with rich national feelings, it will fail if the dancers do not realize it properly. They must clearly understand the characteristics of Korean dance and produce excellent dances which are lifelike, beautiful and full of national emotions by making the best use of their characteristics.

Singers who take part in an opera should become experts in singing, acting and dancing. They should acquire the ability to perform any task at any time if it is assigned to them. Practical skill is acquired in the course of uninterrupted practice and creation. Through practice and creation singers should improve their skill continuously and continue to study to attain a higher standard.

2) THE MUSICAL INTERPRETATION DEPENDS ON THE CONDUCTOR

The interpretation of orchestral music for an opera is not only a task for the composer but also a common task for the conductor and the performers. The performance of a song in an opera is the product of the concerted efforts of the composer, conductor and singers, whereas an orchestral performance is a product of the concerted efforts of the composer, conductor and musicians. The composer should compose an excellent piece of orchestral music which suits the scenes on the stage, and the conductor and musicians should complete it to make it a living musical interpretation.

Exploring the depth of the musical world is the first process of orchestral interpretation. The study of a piece of orchestral music can be effective only when it is begun with the concept of the music and deepened to experience the life it reflects. The content of a piece of music is the life of the character and his thoughts and feelings. The conductor and performers must conduct a close study of the characters' lives and their mental depths so as to form a correct understanding of the music and create a rich interpretation.

If orchestral music is conducted and performed in a perfunctory manner without any close understanding of the life on the stage and without any passion, the performance will not vibrate with the breath of a living man.

The conductor and musicians must grasp the characters' personalities and experience their thoughts and feelings as deeply and truthfully as the actors do and, immersed in the world of their lives, conduct and play their instruments enthusiastically with the characters' feelings. The conducting and the playing of instruments are, in nature, a matter of the heart, just like other creative activities. Their hearts should burn and they should be full of passion for producing orchestral music which moves the audience. Even the music of a large-scale orchestra will be dry, void and unkind to the ear unless it is conducted and played with passion. A small-scale orchestra, if it performs with passion, will surpass the sound of a large orchestra. Success depends not on the scale of instrumentation but on the enthusiasm of the conductor and musicians. When they unanimously accept the characters' minds and conduct and perform the music with passion, the orchestra will resound and draw the audience deep into the drama.

The conductor and musicians must have fertile imaginations and high skill as well as creative passion. The conducting and playing of instruments is not a mechanical art of reproduction but an art of an original and idiomatic musical interpretation. If music is reproduced mechanically on the pretext of preserving its original ideological and artistic qualities, no success can be achieved in conducting and performing it. The conductor and musicians should make the music fresh and idiomatic. Conducting and performing can only be called creative when they sustain the ideological and artistic qualities of the music idiomatically by means of strong imagination and high skill, based on the musical score. They should acquire creative vision and high skill that is capable of making the thoughts and emotions of the music more impressive, as well as a strong imagination that can picture ten images by listening to a sound and measure the whole interpretation by a single part of a melody.

The creative work of the conductor and musicians bears fruit in orchestral resonance. They must study, and have vision and skill which are needed to create a harmonious orchestral interpretation. An orchestral interpretation is created through the artistic harmony of a variety of sounds produced by various instruments. The sounds of individual instruments will produce artistic meaning only when they are harmonious. Harmonious performance is all the more important for the orchestra of our new operas because it is a mixed one of our national and Western instruments.

The harmony of performance can be realized by unifying the methods of the musicians. If our national and Western instruments are played by their own methods of playing, not only can the harmony of the orchestra not be realized but also the distinctive features of the mixed orchestra of our style cannot be sustained. It is a basic way for harmonizing the playing of instruments to unify the methods of playing them.

The instruments of different groups, to say nothing of the instruments in the same group, should be played in a unified manner. Our musicians must acquire our own method of producing a soft, elegant and clear sound. Whatever musical piece they play on whatever instrument, they must sustain the musical emotions by our own method of playing instruments and thus harmonize the orchestral interpretation.

For the harmonious performance of instruments, it is important to coordinate the musicians' postures and movements when they play. This is a prerequisite for unifying the methods of playing and realizing the harmony of the orchestra. Just as the postures and movements of dancers are a part and parcel of the harmony of a dance, so the postures and movements of musicians are an element of a harmonious orchestral performance. If their postures and movements are not coordinated their performance will be disorderly and the instruments will not produce an even sound. All the musicians, when playing, should perform in a unified and unaffected manner in keeping with the sequence of the music.

The harmony of performance is not realized by skill alone. True harmony in the creative team is possible when all the musicians breathe with the same thought and the same emotion. Musicians should breathe with the same thought and the same feeling so as to coordinate their methods of playing their instruments as well as their playing postures and movements.

When they perform, some musicians play their instruments enthusiastically, penetrating the musical piece in harmony with the other musicians but, when they do not perform, they sit idle. This is wrong. An interval during the performance is, in essence, a pause in the context of the musical sequence. So the musicians, whether they are playing or not, must always remain immersed in the world of the music and keep breathing the same air with one another, following the musical sequence.

In opera, harmony between the orchestra and the stage songs and harmony between the orchestra and the *pangchang* must be realized, in addition to the harmony of the orchestra itself.

If the orchestral music is to harmonize with the stage songs, the conductor and musicians must not only meet the technical requirements of accompaniment but also keep breathing the same air with the stage. Many characters with different personalities and aspirations appear on the stage. Therefore, to which character's breathing the orchestral performance is tuned decides whom the orchestral music represents and what thought and emotion it emphasizes. This means that the conductor and musicians must have a principle in following the breathing on the stage.

The conductor and musicians must mainly follow the principal character's breathing throughout the whole context of the stage performance and that of the most significant character in each scene. They must penetrate the depths of the principal and major characters and breathe with them while conducting and performing. Only then can they provide an orchestral interpretation that resounds naturally in step with the events developing on the stage.

The conductor is at the centre of the musical interpretation in opera. He is the commander of the musical interpretation. He must not only be an artist who interprets a musical piece but also an ideological educator and an organizer who inspires the singers and musicians with political awareness and creative passion and organizes their creative work.

In order to fulfil his responsibility and role as commander, the conductor must discard the system and method of arbitrary conducting by which he damps the creativity of the singers and musicians and imposes his will upon them, not allowing any suggestions about the musical interpretation. He must do away with the outmoded system and method of creative work once and for all and establish a new one by which the singers and musicians perform their tasks with an attitude and point of view befitting masters. He must help and lead all the opera singers and musicians so that they, as one, carry out their tasks at the highest level by displaying high political consciousness and responsibility and burning creative zeal.

It is important for the conductor in his work to analyse the musical score in depth and, on the basis of this, draw up a detailed plan of interpretation and coordinate the views on the plan of the members of the creative team.

When drawing up a plan of interpretation, the conductor must not copy the musical score in its entirety but supplement and perfect what has been half-done or overlooked in the process of composition and arrangement and thus confirm the direction of the operatic representation. He must discuss his plan and intentions collectively with the singers and musicians. When discussing the plan he should guide the singers and musicians correctly and see that they advance their opinions fully, reach a consensus of opinion on the musical interpretation and study new ways and means of perfecting the score in an idiomatic way.

After drawing up a detailed plan through collective discussion, he should direct their training in a systematic and scientific manner. Strengthening individual and group training is a prerequisite for raising the standard of the interpretation of the musical score and making it harmonious. In their training the singers and musicians should make it a rule to hold intensive individual training prior to team training and rehearsal.

During a performance, the conductor himself must penetrate the depth of the music; he must also lead the singers and musicians to do the same and at all times breathe the same air with them. He must conduct them by showing the stresses accurately so that they can sing and play with confidence and, in particular, he should lead them to keep the correct tempo.

Maintaining an exact tempo in the playing of instruments is an important factor in the creation of orchestral music as well as in the overall image of the opera. The tempo of the development of the drama depends largely on the performance of the singers, but since the singers sing and act to the orchestral music, their performance is bound to the tempo of the instrumental performance. The tempo of the dramatical development is decided by how the conductor regulates the tempo of the instrumental performance. He must keep a correct standard tempo in the performance of the orchestra to match the general development of the drama.

The standard tempo is the one agreed upon by all the singers, musicians, and stage technicians on the basis of the content of the drama, so the conductor must neither quicken nor reduce it. If the tempo is not kept to exactly, the overall flow of the stage, such as the appearance and exit of the singers, the replacement of the stage sets and backdrops and the change of lighting will become disorderly and, as a result, the artistic harmony of the opera will not be achieved. It is only when he maintains the standard tempo of the instrumental performance that the conductor can give a unified lead to the activities of all the members of the creative team and coordinate the different processes of their creative work.

He must respect the singers and musicians as the masters of the performance of opera music, give full rein to their awareness and creativity, and thus lead them so that they, by themselves, understand the musical score and carry out their creative work properly. He must set a high goal for the musical performance and make strong demands on them. He must combine education and control by teaching them and requiring them to perform as they have been taught so as to give full play to their awareness and creativity.

The conductor, who teaches and leads others, must be better prepared ideologically and artistically than anyone else and acquire great skill in conducting. Only an able conductor can fulfil his duty and role as the commander of the musical interpretation.

3) THE DIRECTOR IS RESPONSIBLE FOR THE HARMONY OF THE STAGE

The director plays a major role in the production of an opera. The director is as much the commander in operatic production as he is in film production. He is the commander who gives a unified lead to all the branches of operatic production, including the music, whereas the conductor is the commander of the musical interpretation alone.

The director is responsible for giving unified guidance to the artists of the different branches so as to present a literary work on the stage in a vivid and harmonious manner. Moreover, in creating an opera of a new type the content and form of which are fresh and original, the director is faced with new tasks which the creation of a conventional opera did not raise. The new type of opera, unlike the opera of the past, is

171

revolutionary and rich in its content and complicated and varied in its means of portrayal. The director must coordinate a variety of interpretations created by individual artists to accord with the requirements of the seed and the distinctive features of the work and thus create a new artistic portrayal which is harmonious and fresh, integrated and unified.

A core is indispensable in portrayal. The seed is the core of an artistic production. An opera, from the portrayal of the characters to all the other interpretations, is based on the seed. The fundamental factor in bringing out the seed of a work is the personalities of the characters. The director must, therefore, construct the dramatic plot and enhance the harmony of portrayal by centring on the characters.

The director must focus his attention on sustaining the portrayal of the characters not only in dealing with conflicts but also in the use of the means of portrayal. The work of the director, such as using a piece of song and dance or filling the stage area and defining the composition, or organizing the sequence of the drama and scene changes, should be done with a view to depicting the characters in bold relief. Excellent harmony on the stage will be achieved only when the director ensures that all the elements of the opera and the dramatic sequence sustain the images of the characters.

In order to organize the drama with the emphasis on characterization, he must delineate the emotions skilfully. The emotional delineation is the basic element in the dramatic organization. An excellent emotional delineation will render it possible to describe the characters' inmost depths, deepen their dramatic relations and breathe life and energy into dramatic progress. However well the events are arranged and however sharply the conflicts are precipitated, the opera will have no emotional appeal unless the characters' emotions are represented skilfully. The opera stage will be full of vitality

172

and touch the heartstrings of the audience only when the events develop and the conflicts are precipitated to suit the emotional sequence.

Delineating emotions skilfully means describing the flow of the emotions truthfully. Such emotional delineation is important in sustaining the overall image of the opera and drawing the audience into the world of the opera.

The delineation of the emotions can be realistic when it accords with the personalities and lives of the characters. Since a person's emotions emanate from his emotional experience of life, it is natural that the emotions should be delineated in accordance with the personalities of the characters and the logic of life.

In dealing with emotions, the complicated and varied emotions a character experiences in his struggle to attain his ideals should be described in an unaffected, natural manner, and the process by which his emotions undergo various changes should be described delicately. While this is done, the main emotion among them should be emphasized. In the case of an individual, a secondary emotion should be subordinated to his main emotion, and in the overall interpretation, the lines of the emotions of secondary characters should be subordinated to that of the principal character. Emotional delineation itself is a method of sustaining the main emotional line, bringing out the essence of a personality and clarifying the main trend of life.

Emotions should be built up in accordance with the characters' personalities and the logic of life, and brought to a head at the right moment. The build-up and climax of the emotions should be alternated to accord with the development of life. This will display the characters' mentalities vividly and help the singers to sing naturally. Opera songs are an expression of the characters' thoughts and feelings based

173

on their experience of life. Therefore, songs should be sung based on the emotional build-up at an appropriate moment, and so arouse a response from the audience.

The build-up of the emotions and the moment they are brought to a head should accord with the logic of life and the sequence of the drama. If the emotions are brought to a head too late, supposedly to wait for their build-up, or if they are brought to a head prematurely, the dramatic sequence will fall flat and the emotional impact will be lost.

It is important in building up the emotions and bringing them to a climax to calculate the emotional sequence carefully in the context of overall dramatic progress. If the delineation of emotions is swayed by individual scenes, the emotional sequence will be broken and the dramatic development will lose its emotional impact. Even though a scene is emotional enough to use a song, another method of portrayal must be employed if the singing disturbs the overall sequence of the emotion so that the emotional sequence does not lapse or break up.

What is important in ensuring a consistent emotional flow is to provide appropriate emotional links between different scenes. In opera the emotional flow is liable to break when the scene changes, so different scenes should be provided with appropriate emotional links. It is only when the emotional flow, as well as the logical sequence, is consistent in spite of the scene changes that the line of emotions will be steady and the drama will continue to develop towards a climax.

Whether the characters' thoughts and feelings are described in depth or not depends entirely on the singers, who create the characters. When a singer has a correct understanding of his character's inmost thoughts and feelings and experiences them deeply, he can interpret them realistically and regulate the flow of his emotions as required by the development of the drama. The director must, therefore, pay attention to working with the singers, particularly the principal singer.

An important aspect of the director's work with the singers is for him to guide them to portray the lives of their characters skilfully in conformity with the characteristics of the operas of a new type. He must ensure that the singers perform their parts after acquiring a correct understanding and deep experience of the personalities of the characters and their lives. In art, the deeper the creator's intentions are implanted in the portrayal so as to avoid producing a crude image, the better. While implanting his creative intentions in every image the creator must ensure that they are revealed in the natural flow of life so as to produce realistic images that arouse a response from the audience. The director must lead the singers to sing, speak and act as naturally as in reality by basing themselves firmly on life.

The director should lead the singers to act realistically and meet the requirements of the emotional delineation. The overall emotional delineation of a work is based on the characters' emotional world created by the singers. The characters' emotional experience of life underlies the overall emotional delineation of an opera. This means that in delineating emotions, the director should pay attention to working with the singers, particularly to sustaining their emotional experience. He should guide the singers to act in such a way that, while expressing the characters' diverse emotions in an unaffected manner, they build up their emotions and bring them to a head as required by their personalities as well as by the overall development of the drama.

Since opera singers portray their characters' personalities and lives mainly by means of songs, the director must pay attention to sustaining their songs. To this end, he must ensure that the singers' actions and facial expressions reveal the thoughts and feelings of the songs truthfully and in good harmony with them. Actions and facial expressions which hamper the proper portrayal of songs must not be tolerated, no matter how impressive they are, and those which, though awkward and unrefined, are helpful to sustaining their songs must be encouraged and perfected.

An operatic portrayal is the product of teamwork. The director must study the libretto with all the creative workers, guide them to accept it as their own production and achieve a consensus of opinion concerning it; only then can he create harmonious interpretation of the opera. The most important thing in establishing a consensus is for the creative workers to have a correct understanding of the seed. It is only when they have a clear understanding of the seed and implement it throughout the whole course of their creative work that the music, dance, stage art and all other artistic branches can become a harmonious entity.

The director must intensify the ideological education of the creative group throughout the operatic production.

An opera reflects the ideological and artistic levels of the creative group. The unity of ideology and will of the group is a precondition for a harmonious operatic interpretation. A harmonious opera cannot be produced by a group in which there is even a slight difference over their understanding and analysis of the work, to say nothing of a group in which the individuals seek personal fame or take to skill-first principles, in disregard of their unity. Only a group whose creative workers all perform their creative work by displaying high skill and breathing and thinking as one on the basis of a single idea and purpose can create a truly harmonious opera.

The ideological education of the creative workers plays a

great role not only in enhancing the ideological and artistic value of the opera and achieving its artistic harmony but also in applying the principle of the speed campaign to the creative work and transforming the creators and artists into revolutionaries. The director should give definite precedence to ideological education in guiding the creative work. He must intensify this education and see that all the creative workers unite firmly in ideology and will, display their energy and knowledge to the full and maintain a high spirit of collectivism. Ideological education is aimed at producing a more excellent work with high ideological and artistic qualities more quickly. The director must, therefore, combine this education closely with the creative work and conduct it without interruption throughout the whole course of the operatic production.

As the commander of the creative group, the director must always set a personal example. Only then can he rally the creative workers as one, lead them properly to bring the seed into full bloom and present on the stage a beautiful, harmonious and wonderful opera.

*   *   *

I have dwelt on the Party's policy on developing the art of opera of our own style and detailed ways and means of carrying it out.

We have been able to effect a revolution in opera successfully and produce five major revolutionary operas, including *The Sea of Blood,* in such a short period because we have been guided by the Party's policy on developing the art of opera and because our artists and writers, who are unfailingly loyal to the Party, have worked with devotion.

177

We should deservedly experience a high sense of national dignity and pride in the fact that, in creating the new *Sea of Blood*-style operas which are fundamentally different from the conventional ones, we have demonstrated their superiority and vitality widely at home and abroad and ushered in the era of revolutionary operas.

We must not, however, rest content with the successes we have achieved. Today we are faced with the task of consolidating and further developing the successes we have achieved in the opera revolution and of further improving the art and literature of our own style.

Our artists and writers, upholding the great leader's ideas on art and literature and their application, the Party's policy on art and literature, must explore the vibrant reality and produce still more operas and other revolutionary works of art and literature, and thus make an active contribution to the modelling of the whole society on the Juche idea. For the immediate period ahead, artists and writers must produce a new, excellent *Sea of Blood*-style opera to mark the 30th anniversary of the foundation of the Workers' Party of Korea and glorify this jubilant anniversary.

I strongly believe that all our artists and writers will remain unfailingly loyal to the Party and the leader and make innovations in the creation of revolutionary works of art and literature.

NOTES

1.   **Pansori**—a kind of song sung in a hoarse voice by Korean aristocrats in the feudal age while drinking. The *pansori*, as a narrative song, was developed mainly in the area of Cholla Province from the latter half of the 18th century through the whole of the 19th century. This song does not cater to the tastes of the people of our times. Its words are too difficult to understand, its tempo is slow and it is weak. Worse still, it is sung in a husky voice which is not pleasing to the ear. Because of these defects it does not excite people nor arouse them to struggle. It is disliked by people, especially by young people.

At present all sectors of musical art are developing our national music on the basis of folk songs instead of the *pansori*.   — p.5

2.   **The Chollima age**—a magnificent period in which our people are building socialism at an unprecedentedly high speed. The word Chollima means a horse which covers thousands of miles a day. This has been used as a term symbolizing high speed from the time of our remote ancestors.

This period began with the great upsurge in socialist construction in our country after the December Plenary Meeting of the Central Committee of the Workers' Party of Korea in 1956.   — p.5

3.   **The speed campaign**—a basic form of fighting for the building of socialism by which all work is performed like lightning.

It is a revolutionary principle to develop work so as to bring about a continuous rapid advance and achieve miraculous successes by relying on the high political awareness and creativity of the popular masses.

The main requirement of the speed campaign is to work as quickly as possible with the mobilization of all forces, while ensuring quality of the highest level.   — p.12

4.   **A lightning operation**—a principle of organizing work by accepting the instructions of the great leader Comrade Kim Il Sung

and the Party's policies sensitively and promptly and carrying them out quickly by mustering all forces. It requires an unprecedentedly high speed in performing one's tasks by tolerating no stagnation. It is a continuous, powerful offensive operation that allows no interruption or hold-up.

This operation involves only continuous, strong and offensive actions and progress to complete an undertaking at an exceptionally high speed. — p.12

CPSIA information can be obtained
at www.ICGtesting.com
Printed in the USA
BVOW04s1145091216
470333BV00001B/1/P